Documents and Debates
the Spanish Civil War

Documents and Debates
General Editor: John Wroughton M.A., F.R.Hist.S.

The Spanish Civil War

Patricia Knight M.A., Ph.D.

Lecturer in History, City and East London College

M
MACMILLAN

First edition 1991

Published by
MACMILLAN EDUCATION LTD
Houndmills, Basingstoke, Hampshire RG21 2XS
and London
Companies and representatives
throughout the world

Printed in Hong Kong

British Library Cataloguing in Publication Data
Knight, Patricia
    The Spanish Civil War. – (Documents and debates)
    1. Spanish Civil War
    I. Title   II. Series
    946.081

    ISBN 0-333-51111-5

Contents

List of Illustrations

The publishers have made every effort to trace the copyright holders but if they have inadvertently overlooked any, they will be pleased to make the necessary arrangement at the first opportunity.

General Editor's Preface

This book forms part of a series entitled *Documents and Debates*, which is aimed primarily at sixth formers. The earlier volumes in the series each covered approximately one century of history, using material both from original documents and from modern historians. The more recent volumes, however, are designed in response to the changing trends in history examinations at 18 plus, most of which now demand the study of documentary sources and the testing of historical skills. Each volume therefore concentrates on a particular topic within a narrow span of time. It consists of eight sections, each dealing with a major theme in depth, illustrated by extracts drawn from primary sources. The series intends partly to provide experience for those pupils who are required to answer questions on documentary material at A-level, and partly to provide pupils of all abilities with a digestible and interesting collection of source material, which will extend the normal textbook approach.

This book is designed essentially for the pupil's own personal use. The author's introduction will put the period as a whole into perspective, highlighting the central issues, main controversies, available source material and recent developments. Although it is clearly not our intention to replace the traditional textbook, each section will carry its own brief introduction, which will set the documents into context. A wide variety of source material has been used in order to give the pupils the maximum amount of experience – letters, speeches, newspapers, memoirs, diaries, official papers, Acts of Parliament, Minute Books, accounts, local documents, family papers, etc. The questions vary in difficulty, but aim throughout to compel the pupil to think in depth by the use of unfamiliar material. Historical knowledge and understanding will be tested, as well as basic comprehension. Pupils will also be encouraged by the questions to assess the reliability of evidence, to recognise bias and emotional prejudice, to reconcile conflicting accounts and to extract the essential from the irrelevant. Some questions, *marked with an asterisk*, require knowledge outside the immediate extract and are intended for further research or discussion, based on the pupil's general knowledge of the period. Finally, we hope that students using this material will learn something of the nature of historical inquiry and the role of the historian.

John Wroughton

Chronological Table of Main Events 1923–1939

1923–30   Primo de Rivera dictatorship in power
April 1931   Municipal elections, flight of Alfonso
XIII, and proclamation of the republic

The Second Republic 1931–36
April 1931–November 1933   Left Republican governments in
power. Church, army and land reform
August 1932   Sanjurjo rising
November 1933–February 1936   Right-wing Republican govern-
ments in power. Reversal of reforms
February 1934   Fusion of Jose Antonio's Falange with the JONS
to form one fascist party
October 1934   Asturias and Barcelona risings and repression
February 1936   Popular Front coalition wins Cortes elections.
Growing political violence and disorder
13 July 1936   Assassination of the monarchist leader, Calvo
Sotelo, in Madrid
17–20 July 1936   Military rising in Morocco and in mainland
Spain

The Civil War, July 1936–March 1939

1936
July   Start of Revolution in the Republican zone, Germany and
Italy begin aid to the Nationalists
September   Largo Caballero becomes Prime Minister of a govern-
ment including Socialists, Communists, left Republicans and
later Anarchists. First meeting of the Non-Intervention Com-
mittee in London
October   Franco becomes head of the Nationalist state.
First Soviet aid reaches the republic
November   Battle for Madrid
The Republican government moves to Valencia

1937
February   The Battle of Jarama
    The fall of Malaga to the Nationalists
March   The Battle of Guadalajara
April   Franco seizes control of the Falange and unites it with the
    Carlists
    Nationalists launch attack on Northern Spain
    Bombing of Basque centre of Guernica
May   Fighting in Barcelona between the Communists/Socialists
    and the POUM/CNT
    Negrin replaces Caballero as Prime Minister of the Republic
June–October   Nationalist conquest of North
July   Republican offensive at Brunete
August   Republican offensive in Aragon at Belchite
December   Republican attack on town of Teruel

1938
February   Nationalists recapture Teruel and advance towards the
    Mediterranean
April   Nationalists reach the Mediterranean, cutting Republican
    zone in two
July–November   Final Republican offensive on the Ebro
September   The Munich Conference

1939
January–February   Nationalists occupy Catalonia
March   Anti-Communist coup by Colonel Casado in Madrid.
    After abortive peace talks the Nationalists occupy Madrid
1 April   Civil War ends

Glossary of Political Terms Used in the Text

(Abbreviations are of the Spanish names)

Carlists:	the traditional monarchist/Catholic party, supporting the claims of Don Carlos, based chiefly in Navarre
Caudillo:	the title given to Franco as leader and Head of State
CEDA:	federation of autonomous right-wing parties set up in 1933 by Gil Robles
Civil Guard:	armed police force established to keep internal order
CNT:	the Anarchist trade union, most numerous in Catalonia and Andalusia
Cortes:	the Spanish Parliament
Esquerra:	the left-wing Catalan political party
FAI:	the Anarchist Federation, the revolutionary political wing of the anarchist movement
Falange:	the Spanish fascist party established by Jose Antonio Primo de Rivera in 1933
Generalidad:	the autonomous government of Catalonia granted by the Republic in 1931
Latifundio:	large landed estates mainly found in Andalusia
Lliga:	the conservative Catalan political party
POUM:	a Marxist, anti-Stalinist party mainly based in Catalonia
PSUC:	Federation of the Communists and Socialists in Catalonia, formed in 1936
Requetes:	Carlist unofficial army or militia, incorporated into the Nationalist army
UGT:	The Socialist trade union, rival to the CNT

The Spanish Civil War

The Spanish Civil War 'captured the imagination of a generation' and still generates enormous interest. Historians have found it impossible to be neutral about the war and most works written in this country have favoured the Republic.

In the 1930s and for some time after, the war was generally perceived in broad ideological terms as part of the wider European struggle between democracy or communism on the one hand and fascism on the other. Intellectuals, writers and poets rushed to take sides, mostly in favour of the Republic, and many also hastened to Spain to participate as combatants or reporters. Well known writers who visited Spain included Ernest Hemingway, George Orwell, Clive Bell and W. H. Auden. As Philip Toynbee saw it, 'the gloves were off in the struggle against fascism', and Stephen Spender commented that 'Spain offered the twentieth century an 1848'. The conflict in Spain was mainly seen not as a Spanish but as a European phenomenon, the opening round in a war against the fascist dictators, a dress rehearsal for the Second World War, 'only the latest and fiercest battle in the European Civil War which had been raging intermittently for the previous twenty years', since the Russian Revolution (Paul Preston).

With this perspective the role of Germany and Italy and of the International Brigades was inevitably exaggerated. It was usual to see the war as resulting from a fascist plot aided and abetted by Hitler and Mussolini, who then used their military might and exploited British and French appeasement to secure Franco in power.

Under Franco's regime original Spanish sources were not always available to researchers and the official Spanish accounts of the war favoured the Nationalists. After Franco's death in 1975 and the coming of democracy to Spain, more research materials became accessible but many Spanish sources, especially on the Nationalist side, are still not available in translation. As a result of these restrictions the most widely read popular accounts of the war in Britain are still those by members of the International Brigades, all written from a Republican and often a Communist perspective. These memoirs are often informative and exciting, but they all tend to cover similar ground, dealing mainly with military campaigns, especially those around Madrid in the early stages of the war. Perhaps the best known, and certainly the best written, is George Orwell's *Homage to Catalonia*, which as well as military events describes the political struggles on the Republican side from a position sympathetic to the Anarchists.

Recently, with wider access to primary sources, historians have adopted different and more varied perspectives. The war has come to be seen as specifically Spanish in its origins and its outcome, a 'fundamentally Spanish affair rooted in the agrarian question and comprehensible only in terms of the previous hundred years of Spanish development' (Paul Preston).

Starting with Hugh Thomas's *Spanish Civil War*, and continuing with volumes by Raymond Carr, Paul Preston and Gabriel Jackson, historians have sought to identify the Spanish features of the Civil War. More detailed attention has been given to Spanish politics in the 1930s, notably in Stanley Payne's works on the Falange and the army, Martin Blinkhorn's research on Carlism, and Burnett Bolloten's volume on the role of the Communist Party in Republican Spain. Recent volumes of essays have focused on local and regional aspects of the war.

In view of the continued interest generated by the Spanish Civil War the dearth of documentary collections is surprising. The exceptions are a selection of documents at the end of H. Browne's very useful volume in the 'Seminar Studies' series and Ronald Fraser's large and comprehensive collection of Spanish eye-witness accounts in *Blood of Spain* (Penguin, 1981).

In this volume I have tried to include a wider variety of sources than has generally been the case. I have also endeavoured to balance the more popular journalistic and International Brigade accounts with less well known Spanish primary sources where these are available in translation, and by including where possible a Nationalist as well as a Republican perspective. Official documents are of course valuable in assessing the opinions of foreign govenments. In particular the *Documents on German Foreign Policy* are a mine of information, not only on German relations with Franco, but on political developments within Nationalist Spain and on the progress of the war.

Few other historical topics have been subject to so much controversy. The most important themes covered in this book centre on the origins of the war, the nature of Franco's regime and the causes of Nationalist success. The issue of why democracy broke down in Spain, and which of the two opposing sides, left or right, bore the greater responsibility for the war has been extensively debated by historians, and the first two chapters of this volume cover Spain under the Republic from 1931 to 1936.

Argument also surrounds the nature of Franco's regime, which is considered in chapter VI. Was he a Fascist modelling himself on the German and Italian dictators, and surviving only because of the windfall of American support in the Cold War period? Or was he simply a conventional military leader, authoritarian rather than totalitarian, who organised an army rising in the tradition of Spanish pronunciamientos, and who cunningly used Hitler and Mussolini to his own advantage rather than theirs?

A third main theme predominating in this volume concerns the reasons for Nationalist victory in the war. Early historians of the Civil War often assumed that Franco won because of German and Italian aid and the lamentable failure of the Western Democracies to assist the Republic. Immediately after the war, on the Republican side the Spanish Communists and their opponents bitterly denounced and blamed one another for their defeat. There is still a lively debate on the internal politics of the Republic and on the effects of Communist influence. Did the Communists help lose the war by stifling the revolution or were they the only efficient force capable of winning it? Burnett Bolloten, in *The Spanish Revolution*, has critically analysed the demoralising Soviet influence over the Republic, whereas other historians consider that the Republic was only kept going by Soviet supplies and by a professionalised popular army dominated by the Communists. Attention has recently shifted from the Republican failures to a closer analysis of the causes of Nationalist success. Historians have looked more closely at Nationalist military organisation, personnel and tactics and concluded that these were superior to those of the Republicans. In the words of Martin Blinkhorn, attention has focused not simply on the quantities of foreign aid but on 'the manner in which foreign aid and influence related to internal political and military considerations'. The politics of Nationalist Spain have also been scrutinised and historians now generally agree that Franco's success in forging political unity was an important factor in his victory and in his continued dominance of Spain until his death in 1975.

I The Origins of the War and the Spanish Republic

Introduction

Historians now agree that the Spanish Civil War had its origins in the previous hundred years of Spanish history and in the long-term conflict between modernising and conservative forces. At the beginning of the twentieth century Spain was still in many respects a feudal society, dominated by landowners, church and army. The rural areas with their population of impoverished peasants and labourers contrasted with industrial regions such as Catalonia, the Basque country and the Asturias, where differing language and culture led to demands for self-government.

In 1923, following a military defeat in Spain's remaining colony of Morocco, a dictatorship was established under General Miguel Primo de Rivera, supported by King Alfonso and the army. Primo's regime, sometimes compared with that of Mussolini in Italy, was short-lived. The effects of the world economic depression and loss of support from the army led to his resignation in 1930. Attempts to replace him failed, and the local elections of April 1931 were won by the Republicans, whose support had been growing since the 1930 Pact of San Sebastian between the middle-class liberals and the socialists. Alfonso left the country and the Republic was established.

But the Republic which was welcomed with enthusiasm and hope in 1931 was on the verge of collapse by the end of 1935. It can be argued that this outcome was to some extent inevitable, 'the social conflicts of a semi-industrialised country were too violent to be contained within a parliamentary framework' (Raymond Carr). But there is also evidence that the Republican governments from 1931–3 made avoidable mistakes. Religious Spaniards were antagonised by Church reform while army reforms left the hard-core of right-wing army officers intact. Agrarian reform was too little, too late, 'An aspirin to cure appendicitis' in the words of the Socialist leader, Largo Caballero, which frightened the middle classes without satisfying the workers.

The dominance of the left-wing liberals and socialists was

challenged by a new Catholic party, the CEDA. This party and its allies the right-wing Republicans gained a majority in the November 1933 Cortes elections, ushering in the so-called 'two black years' when most of the earlier reforms were reversed. The character and aims of the CEDA are controversial. Was it an embryonic fascist party determined to destroy the Republic or 'a genuinely modern Christian democrat party' (Richard Robinson)? A section of the Socialist Party, led by Largo Caballero, believed that the CEDA intended to crush democracy in Spain as Hitler had done in Germany. The entry of three CEDA representatives into the government in October 1934 was the signal for a left-wing rising. This quickly collapsed in Madrid and Barcelona but in the Asturias the miners held Oviedo and the surrounding areas for two weeks. The rising has been described as 'the first battle of the Civil War'. Its aftermath and particularly the harsh suppression by Moorish troops bitterly polarised Spanish politics and a section of the Socialist Party led by Largo Caballero became increasingly revolutionary.

The questions a historian must ask are when and why a democratic republic acceptable to most Spaniards became impossible. Did the Republic fail because the privileged classes refused to concede reasonable reforms, or was the left to blame for being the first to resort to an armed rising in 1934? 'The right', says Paul Preston, 'in blocking change so exasperated the working class as to undermine their faith in parliamentary democracy. Once that happened and once the left turned to revolutionary solutions, the right's determination to destabilise the Republic would be enormously facilitated.'

1   Social and political conflict

(a) Map of regional and political divisions (see page 6)

(b) The land problem in Spain

There exist two main agrarian problems in Spain: that of the small holdings in the centre and the north which are sometimes too small to maintain the men who work on them, and that of the large estates in the south, which are run by a factory system that keeps
5   down wages to starvation point by means of huge reserves of unemployed labour.

Andalusia is the classic land of latifundia or large estates. An English or French town that has 12,000 inhabitants is a busy place. Not so an Andalusian pueblo of the same size. The first impression
10   is one of decay and stagnation. A few wretched shops selling only the bare necessities of life: one or two petty industries – soap

(a) Regional and political divisions in Spain

making, weaving of mats, potteries, oil distilleries that between
them employ some couple of hundred men: the ancestral houses of
the absentee landowners, dilapidated and falling into ruins: then a
few bourgeois families – the overseers of the large estates or the
farmers who rent from them . . . and then the landless proletariat.
Three-quarters of the population consists of these men and their
families who are hired by the day, by the month, by the season, –
rarely for longer than that . . . In 1930 they were earning on
average from 3 to 3.5 pesetas (1s 6d to 1s 9d), for an eight hour day
during four or five months of the year. For four, five or six months
of the year they are unemployed . . . they would starve but for the
credit given by the shops . . . .

During the war it paid landowners to cultivate the whole of their
estates but since 1918 the area of uncultivated land inevitably began
to grow again. . . . The average aristocrat living in Madrid or
Seville simply took the advice of his steward and did not bother his
head about estates where he knew no-one by sight and which he
regarded very much as if they were some distant colony. When for
example, the Duke of Alba who has not got the reputation of being
a bad landlord, visited his ancestral acres, he did so with an
equipment of lorries and tents as though he were travelling in the
centre of Africa.

> Gerald Brenan, *The Spanish Labyrinth* (Cambridge, CUP,
> 1943), pp 118–19

(c) Catalonia

Spain is the impoverished agrarian tyrant while Catalonia is the rich
industrial rebel. . . Catalonia accounts for about ten per cent of all
Spanish agricultural production but for 87 per cent of industrial
production.

> Frank Jellinek, *The Civil War in Spain*, quoted in H. Purcell,
> *The Spanish Civil War* (London, Wayland, 1973), p 23

(d) The Catholic Catechism, 1927

What does Liberalism teach?
That the State is independent of the Church.
What kind of sin is Liberalism?
It is a most grievous sin against faith.
Why?
Because it consists in a collection of heresies condemned by the
Church.
Is it a sin for a Catholic to read a Liberal newspaper?
He may read the Stock Exchange News.

What sin is generally committed by him who votes for a Liberal
candidate?
Generally a mortal sin.
> Quoted in Brenan, *Spanish Labyrinth*, pp 51–2

(e) Anarchist beliefs

50 We at the FAI were idealogues, but the CNT was a purely trade
union movement. We were not a political party, we despised
governments and politicians. Our goal was to redeem the exploited
workers. Our workers clubs educated people for better lives,
dignified the workers. The FAI was clandestine. Not even my
55 comrades knew my real name. Once the civil guards came to our
house. Lola shouted and I escaped. The organisation sent me to
Brussels where I was joined by Durruti and Acaso. With the money
from their bank raids in South America we opened a libertarian
bookshop in Paris and financed an anarchist encyclopaedia.
60   When I met libertarians I was accepted as a human being. It was
like a religious conversion . . . there was a strong puritan streak in
anarchist philosophy. We didn't smoke or drink. Many of us were
vegetarians. We didn't get married in church, we just went to live
with a comrade.
> Anarchist quoted in D. Mitchell, *Spanish Civil War*, (Lon-
> don, Granada, 1982), p 10

(f) The Spanish Socialists

65 For a long time the Socialists remained very small – just a few
thousand members with its main strength in Madrid. The
overwhelming majority of industrial workers in the industrial
centres and in the countryside remained anarchist for decades. The
Socialists strove not for social equality but for the betterment of the
70 workers. Their leaders loved the detail, the procedure, the routine.
Punctilious administration was their main strength. They hated
anything new, young and violent . . . . In 1932 a memorandum of
the UGT showed that in three and a half years they had spent
200,000 pesetas on administration and only 15,000 pesetas for
75 assistance to prisoners.
> Edward Conze, *Spain Today, Revolution and Counter-
> revolution* (London, 1936), pp 51–2

Questions

a What evidence does extract *a* provide of the regional and
political conflicts of Spain in the early 1930s?
b Why had it paid landowners to cultivate their estates during the
war and why after 1918, had land again been left uncultivated
(extract *b*, lines 24–6)?

c Explain the statement, 'Spain is the impoverished agrarian tyrant while Catalonia is the rich industrial rebel', lines 34–7.

d Why do you think the Church exempted the Stock Exchange News from the ban on liberal newspapers (lines 45–6)?

e 'Spain entered the 1930s a backward state' (Browne). Discuss this statement in the light of extracts *b, c,* and *d.*

f Identify the CNT (line 50), the FAI (line 50), the UGT (line 74). Identify from extract *a* the main areas of support of the CNT and UGT and explain the regional differences in their strength.

g Why do you think the FAI was 'clandestine' (line 54)?

h What do extracts *e* and *f* reveal of the differences in beliefs and methods between the Anarchists and the Socialists?

i What evidence is there in extract *f* to indicate that the author is critical of the Socialists and the UGT?

2 The dictatorship of Primo de Rivera 1923–1930

Two contemporary accounts of Primo's regime

(a) Primo de Rivera started his job as dictator under the most favourable auspices that ever inaugurated a dictatorship. His programme was contained in two sentences . . . destroy the old political parties and reorganise the state by modernising the
5 country. In the six years of his dictatorship he did as much to achieve the second task as could possibly be expected. What elements of modern life there are today in Spain mostly date from the time of Primo. The Republicans are loath to acknowledge it. But wherever there is a splendid road [and there are many], a
10 modern inn in a small town, a new breakwater at some important port, a modern barracks or a modern prison, in nine out of ten cases it will have been constructed under Primo's administration. . . .

For the first time in Spanish history a constructive effort was made to solve the 'social problem'. Compulsory collective bargain-
15 ing was introduced in order to secure acceptable wages for the workers. . . . The UGT was only too glad to accept this unexpected gift, it was recognised officially as a partner in collective bargaining, and while all the other parties were persecuted, the Socialists were tolerated.

> Frank Borkenau, *The Spanish Cockpit* (London, Faber, 1937), p 40

20 **(b)** The achievements of the dictatorship were numerous and in their way very important, but compared with its failures, super-ficial . . . prosperity was solely material and began to disappear as taxation increased; the peseta dropped . . . free speech and free

expression of opinion were done away with; had it been possible to do away with free thought the dictatorship would doubtless have been functioning to this day; newspapers were censored and suspended, public meetings and even banquets policed with spies, leading men fined, imprisoned or exiled for the mildest indiscretion; clubs closed, universities suspended for indefinite periods. Of all the Dictator's tyrannies, the most flagrant was probably his treatment of Catalonia. The small concessions made to regional autonomy were abolished, the use of the Catalan language at public meetings was prohibited.

Allison Peers, *The Spanish Tragedy* (London 1937), p 4

Questions

a   Explain the reference to Catalan regional autonomy (lines 31–2).
★ b   In what circumstances had Primo come to power in 1923?
c   To what extent can the two accounts of Primo's regime be reconciled?
d   What light do these two extracts throw on the reasons for Primo's fall from power in 1930?

3 The establishment of the Republic, April 1931

(a) The abdication of Alfonso

The municipal election results presented real difficulty if any attempt at repression were made. In the scores of towns and villages where Republican-Socialist councillors had a majority these men were all taking possession and hoisting the Republican flag over the town halls. But for the Government after holding the elections [to find out which way the wind was blowing], to have ordered the Civil Guard to bar the doors to the town halls and to have fired on the angry crowds which would have protested, would have been too illogical a proposition. The Prime Minister summed the matter up when he said, 'Spain woke up Republican this morning'. . . .

Negotiations [on the future of the monarchy] were carried on in the salon of the house of a close personal friend of the monarch. Alcala Zamora was quite adamant: 'The King must leave before sunset'. The King walked out into an ante-chamber where various Cabinet Ministers, grandees and other personalities were gathered. A dashing cavalry officer, General Marquess of Cavalcanti, said, 'Sire I offer you the full support of my troops to defend your throne'. General Berenguer immediately cut in with a sharp, 'Prove what you say; prove that it is possible to restore order by bringing out troops before making such sweeping statements'. Cavalcanti was about to answer back angrily but Don Alfonso intervened

sadly saying, 'There is no need at all for discussion my friends, my
mind is quite made up and I shall leave the country tonight'. In
25 observance of the Republican ultimatum shortly before dusk five or
six powerful cars swung out of the private entrance to the palace
grounds and twelve hours later the King was sailing for Marseilles
on the cruiser *Jaime I*.

While Don Alfonso was sadly deciding which way to leave, Sn.
30 Alcala Zamora and his colleagues set out for the Ministry of the
Interior. Their cars wedged their way through the delirious crowds
at a speed which would make snail's pace seem like the Grand Prix
in comparison. The big wooden doors were shut and bolted. Bang,
bang, bang, smote Sn. Zamora and he called lustily on the guard
35 within to 'open in the name of the Republic'. Civil Guards swung
back the doors and Zamora and his friends were swept up the stairs
on a tidal wave of enthusiastic supporters. The key ministry was in
Republican hands without a drop of blood being shed.

> Henry Buckley (a reporter for the *Daily Chronicle*) *The Life
> and Death of the Spanish Republic* (London, Hamish Hamil-
> ton, 1940), pp 38–42

(b) Alfonso's Manifesto, 14 April 1931

The Elections which took place on Sunday show me clearly that I
40 no longer have the love of my people. My conscience tells me that
this indifference will not be final for I have always done my utmost
to serve Spain. I am King of all Spaniards and I am also myself a
Spaniard. I could find ample means to maintain my royal
prerogative by making effective use of force against those who
45 contest it . . . but I desire most resolutely to abstain from any
course which might plunge my compatriots into a fratricidal civil
war. I renounce none of my rights for they are not so much my
own as a trust committed to me by History. I await the tidings of
the authentic and adequate expression of the nations' collective
50 conscience and while the nation is speaking I deliberately suspend
the exercise of royal powers and leave Spain.

> Peers, *Spanish Tragedy*, pp 45–6

Questions

a   Who were Zamora (line 14), Berenguer (line 19)? What was the
    Civil Guard (line 7)?
b   What evidence is there in extract *a* to support the view that
    'Spain woke up Republican'?
c   What is meant in the context of the extract by the phrases 'royal
    prerogative' (lines 43–4), and 'a trust committed to me by
    History' (line 48)?
d   What impression did Alfonso intend to convey and what did he
    expect to achieve by issuing the Manifesto reproduced in extract
    b?

4 The Republic and the Church 1931–1933

(a) Cardinal Segura's Pastoral Letter, May 1931

We gratefully remember His Majesty King Alfonso XIII who during his reign successfully preserved the ancient traditions and piety of his ancestors. In these months of terrible uncertainty every Catholic must measure the magnitude of his responsibilities and
5   valiantly perform his duty. . . . If we remain 'quiet and idle'; if we allow ourselves to give way to 'apathy and timidity'; if we leave open the way to those who are attempting to destroy religion, or if we expect the benevolence of our enemies to secure the triumph of our ideals, we shall have no right to lament when bitter reality
10 shows us that we had victory in our hands yet knew not how to fight like intrepid warriors prepared to succumb gloriously.

Quoted in Peers, *Spanish Tragedy*, pp 52–3

(b) A Republican youth leader's view

What a provocation the monarchist meeting was! Only weeks after the proclamation of the republic, which had happened so peacefully that anyone who wanted could go to mass! The next day several
15 convents were burnt but not a single priest, friar or nun was killed. Under the monarchy in the last century not only did convents burn but priests were massacred. No, the fact of the matter was that the Spanish right had its roots in clericalism, was a 'religious' oligarchy; but it was a religion that had nothing to do with
20 Christianity.

Quoted in Ronald Fraser, *Blood of Spain* (Harmondsworth, Penguin, 1981), p 527

(c) Azana's speech in the Cortes debate on church reform, 13 October 1931

Today Spain has ceased to be Catholic despite the fact that there are millions of Spaniards who are practising Catholics . . . the continual influence of the religious orders on the conscience of the young is the situation which as Republicans we are in duty bound
25 at all costs to prevent. Do not tell me that this is contrary to freedom; it is a question of public health. Would you, who opposes this measure in the name of liberalism permit a university professor to lecture on astronomy and to say that the stars are fastened in the spheres which make up the heavens? I tell you that the Catholic
30 religious orders are compelled by virtue of their dogma to teach everything that is contrary to the principles which are the foundation of the modern state.

Peers, *Spanish Tragedy*, pp 71–3

a Why would Cardinal Segura's pastoral letter (extract *a*) be likely to alarm and antagonise republicans?

b Explain the last sentence of extract *b*.

c How adequate do you find Azana's justification of church reform given in extract *c*?

★ *d* How far do you agree with the view that the anti-clericalism of the Republican Government was 'political folly' (Thomas)?

5 Republican land reform in Andalusia

An estate called La Reina near Cordoba owned by the Duke of Medinecali was handed over to the inhabitants of a nearby hamlet. What joy there was in Santa Cruz that day! Soon sixty-two settlers were in occupation of the large farm. I was very interested in
5 agrarian reform, convinced the only solution was to work the land collectively and I often went to La Reina to see how things were going. . . . The Institute of Agrarian Reform decided the estate should be worked collectively and each settler was given a mule to be paid for in due course.
10 When the ploughing started many of the settlers began to say that others' mules were being worked less hard than their own and that there was favouritism. I went to the estate one day; there was an hour to go before the work day ended. Twenty-five teams were ploughing – if you could call it that. Each was running almost in
15 the furrow of the plough ahead.
The mistake was to have allocated the mules individually and then expect them to work in common. . . . Soon there were complaints that the foremen whom the settlers had elected weren't working like the rest of the men. The complaints were ridiculous.
20 The foreman worked when he could, but he had to attend to other duties for which he had been elected: keeping the accounts, reporting to the Institute agronomists who came out once or twice weekly from Cordoba. Moreover if the settlers didn't like them they could elect other managers. Instead they preferred to grumble.
25 The trouble was that everyone wanted to be a boss. . . .
The following year the settlers decided to work their plots individually . . . the fact is that they were all worse off. Even more ridiculous was the fact that specialists in different agricultural jobs were now having to do everything on their own plot . . . for all
30 that, the settlers were a lot better off than they had been before the 1932 law. Their houses were bursting with wheat; 1934 was a magnificent year. Some managed to make enough to buy their house and even a bit of land.

Felipe Posadas, a peasant in Santa Cruz, quoted in Fraser, *Blood of Spain*, pp 519–21

Questions

a   What was meant by working the land 'collectively' (line 8)?
b   What evidence is there in the extract that the writer supported
    collectives, rather than individual holdings?
c   This extract is an eyewitness account written several years after
    the event. Assess its value and limitations as evidence for the
    historian.
★ d   What agrarian reforms other than that described in this extract
    had the Republican governments introduced and how success-
    ful had they been?

6 The reaction from the right

(a) Gil Robles on the aims of the CEDA

I speak to the powerful, to those who have plenty to lose, and I say
to them – if you had sacrificed a small sum at the right moment,
you would lose less than you might now, because what you give
for the press, the rightist press, which defends the fundamental
5   principles of every society – religion and family, order, work – is a
real insurance policy for your personal fortune . . . the danger
which threatens our altars also threatens our pockets.

When the social order is threatened Catholics should unite to
defend it and safeguard the principles of Christian civilisation
10 . . . we are faced with a social revolution; in the political panorama
of Europe I can see only the formation of Marxist and anti-Marxist
groups. This is what is happening in Germany and in Spain also.

We must give Spain a true unity, a new spirit, a totalitarian polity
. . . it is necessary now to defeat Socialism inexorably. We must
15 found a new state, purge the fatherland of judaising freemasons . . .
what does it matter if we have to shed blood! We need full power
and that is what we are going to demand . . . to realise this ideal
we are not going to waste time with archaic forms. Democracy is
not an end but a means to the conquest of the new state. When the
20 time comes either parliament submits or we will eliminate it
. . . we are going to parliament to defend our ideals, but if
parliament is against our ideals we shall go against parliament,
because in politics not the forms but the content is what interests
us.

> Extracts from speeches by Gil Robles, February–October
> 1933, quoted in Paul Preston, *The Spanish Civil War*
> (London, Weidenfeld & Nicolson, 1986), p 31. Paul
> Preston, *The Coming of the Spanish Civil War* (London,
> Methuen, 1983) p 48, and Paul Preston (ed.), *The Revolution
> and the War in Spain* (London, Methuen, 1984), p 39

(b) The programme of the Falange, November 1934

25 2. Spain is an indivisible entity in universal terms. Any plot against this indivisible whole is repulsive. All separatism is a crime we shall not forgive.
3. We are committed to the empire. We declare that Spain's historical fulfilment is the empire. We demand for Spain a
30 prominent position in Europe. . . .
6. Ours will be a totalitarian state in the service of the fatherland's integrity. All Spaniards will play a part therein through their membership of families, municipalities and trade unions. The system of political parties will be resolutely abolished, together
35 with inorganic suffrage, representation by conflicting factions and the Cortes as we know it. . . .
10. We reject the capitalist system which disregards the needs of the people, dehumanises private property and transforms the workers into shapeless masses prone to misery and despair. . . .
40 12. The primary purpose of wealth is to effect an improvement in the standard of living of all the people – it is intolerable that great masses of people live in poverty while a few enjoy luxury. . . .
19. We shall achieve a social organisation of agriculture by means of the following measures: by redistributing all the arable land so as
45 to promote family holdings. . . .
25. Our movement integrates the Catholic religion – traditionally glorious and predominant in Spain – into national reconstruction.
26. The Spanish Falange wants the establishment of a new order
. . . so that it may prevail in the conflict with the present order, the
50 Spanish Falange aims at a national revolution. Its style will be trenchant, ardent and militant. Life is a militia and must be lived in a spirit purified by service and sacrifice.

> From Hugh Thomas (ed.), *Jose Antonio Primo de Rivera, Selected Writings* quoted in H. Browne, *Spain's Civil War* (London, Longman, 1983), pp 89–92

(c) The right-wing parties and the 1933 Cortes election

I sat in Robles' ante-room waiting to get news of the campaign. Money was being spent on propaganda on a scale unknown in
55 Spain. Large printing shops worked night and day for weeks on work for the CEDA alone. The massive six story building of *El Debate* (the CEDA newspaper), which was also the head-quarters of the CEDA, literally teemed with people. There were people of every social class. In the next room to me Robles was sitting with a
60 commission of Monarchists. They along with the leader of the Traditionalists were now sitting with Robles, elaborating on election co-operation. In some places they would go in coalition, in other parts one or the other would abstain. Meanwhile an endless

crowd filed by me. Women predominated. There were also noisy
65 young men, smartly dressed with small and cultivated moustaches.
Buckley, *Life and Death of the Spanish Republic,* p 111

Questions

a   Explain the reference to 'what is happening in Germany' (line
13).
b   What is meant by 'purge the fatherland of judaising freemasons'
(line 16)?
c   To what extent does extract *a* support the view that the CEDA
was a fascist party?
d   Explain point 2 of the Falange programme.
e   What is meant by 'inorganic suffrage' (line 35)?
f   Compare and contrast the aims of the CEDA in extract *a* with
the programme of the Falange in extract *b*.
g   How practical was point 3 of the programme of the Falange in
the light of Spain's recent history?
h   Identify 'Monarchists' (line 60) and 'Traditionalists' (line 61).
i   What reasons are given in extract *c* to explain the success of the
right-wing parties in the November 1933 election?

7 Two views of the Asturias Rising, October 1934

(a) It seems very certain that if he could have chosen, Largo
Caballero would have preferred the strictly constitutional parliamentary way for he is a typical reformist leader . . . whether from
conviction, expediency or from a natural desire to retain his
5   influence with the rank and file, after the elections of 1933 he
changed his political tactics. He was bitterly denouncing the sham,
shadow institutions of democracy, declaring that if the Republic
was to be saved, the road must be closed to fascism and that this
would not be achieved by mere parliamentary action.
10   On the 4 October Lerroux announced that three fascists, the
nominees of Gil Robles, had been taken into his new Cabinet. That
evening the general strike began in the Asturias; it became almost
immediately an armed rising . . . in every section of the towns, in
every village, Soviets of workers and peasants were formed.
15   Among the decrees passed were those abolishing private owner-
ship of the means of production and abolishing rent. All communications were cut, the railway blockaded and Oviedo the government centre seized and held by the revolutionary forces. Oviedo
possessed two large armaments factories. From this source the
20   miners availed themselves of 20,000 rifles, hundreds of machine
guns, several pieces of light artillery, some armoured cars and an

armoured train. For nine days they held the town against the combined efforts of the military garrison, the civil guard and the assault guards and against the foreign legion and arab army corps
25 which had landed in Gijon and were advancing on the town . . . in Mieres [a mining village] the miners entered the village without firing a single shot and proclaimed a peasant and workers government. The leaders gave out vouchers for the acquiring of provisions and shared them out among the inhabitants. Money was
30 abolished and a Red Guard formed. The arsenal of arms was prepared in the church but they did not do the slightest harm to the priest.

> Leah Manning, *What I Saw in Spain* (London, Gollancz, 1935) pp 89–112 (an account based on a visit to Spain a few weeks after the Rising)

(b) The excuse to set the movement going was the solution announced for the ministerial crisis of the beginning of October
35 . . . those who objected to the ministerial participation of Popular Action were the extreme left group, who had become enemies of the regime from the moment when the republic ceased to obey their wishes.

The Socialists since their fall from power had proclaimed
40 themselves enemies of the 'bourgeois Republic' which they had supported in 1931. Now they hurled themselves against it with violence to conquer 'all power to the proletariat' by means of a bloody revolution.

The town of Oviedo was insufficiently garrisoned by less than
45 1,000 men belonging to the army and assault guards clumsily distributed over official centres and a few strategic points . . . these dispositions permitted an avalanche of invaders, some 8,000 miners, perfectly armed and using dynamite with skill and courage, to seize most of the town on the night of 5th October. . . . It was a
50 very cruel battle . . . more than 110 houses, the finest in the town, were burned or blown up, including buildings such as the university (where in the destructions of its magnificent library the accumulated treasures of 4 centuries were lost. . . . The civil population underwent all the horrors of war and revolution
55 combined. . . . Nine terrible days passed without light, without water, with scarcely any food. . . . Red guards entered the houses through shattered doors or broken windows, molesting, imprisoning and shooting at pleasure. The greatest cruelty was shown to priests and nuns. About 40 were killed in the Asturias.

> Alfred Mendizabal, *The Martyrdom of Spain* (London, Geoffrey Bles, 1938), pp 207–11 (an eyewitness account by a professor of law at Oviedo University)

Questions

a   Who were the 'assault guards' (line 24), the 'foreign legion and arab army corps' (line 24)? Identify Largo Caballero (lines 1–2).
b   Explain the sentence 'sham, shadow institutions of democracy . . . mere parliamentary action' (lines 6–9).
c   Why did the miners set up 'Soviets of workers and peasants' (line 14)?
d   What 'ministerial crisis' is referred to in line 34?
e   In what ways do extracts *a* and *b* differ in their view of the policies of Largo Caballero?
f   On what points do extracts *a* and *b* agree in their description of the Rising?
g   What does the language and content of extracts *a* and *b* reveal of the political sympathies of their authors?

8 The Republic in danger

(a) A conversation with Franco, January 1936

General Franco seemed very worried about the situation, but we never had an opportunity to talk properly until we were on our way back. There was a storm in the Channel. Franco said, 'Let's go up on deck'. The deck was deserted. He took me behind a
5   smokestack where there was some shelter from the wind. 'Now we can talk', he said, and he told me all about the Comintern meeting [July 1935, where the Popular Front strategy had been agreed] and how like him there were other officers who were worried – Mola and Goded and so on – and Sanjurjo was being kept informed. He
10 said that of course the Popular Front hadn't yet won the elections, but that he believed they would. Again, it all depended on what the Popular Front did if they won. But the army had to be prepared. If the worst came to the worst, then it would be our duty to intervene. If the Popular Front won, of course, he would not be
15 kept on as Chief-of-Staff. I said I was at his disposal. He said I was to remain in Paris – 'if you hear of me going to Africa, you'll know we have decided there's no other way but a rising'.

> A conversation with the Spanish military attache in Paris in January 1936 while returning from the funeral of George V. Quoted in George Hill, *Franco* (London, Robert Hale, 1967) p 210

(b) Largo Caballero's view

Our duty is to establish Socialism. And when I speak of Socialism I speak of Marxist Socialism. And when I speak of Revolutionary

20   Socialism our aspiration is the conquest of political power. By what
means? Those we are able to use! Let it be well understood that by
going with the left Republicans we are mortgaging absolutely
nothing of our ideology and action . . . it is an alliance, a
circumstantial coalition, for which a programme is being prepared
25   that is certainly not going to satisfy us, but I say here and now to
those present and to all those who can hear and read that . . .
everyone united must fight to defend. . . . Do not be dismayed, do
not be disheartened if you do not see things in the programme
which are absolutely basic to our ideology. No! That must never be
30   a reason for ceasing to work with complete faith and enthusiasm
for victory . . . that way comrades, after victory, and freed of
every kind of commitment, we shall be able to say to everyone that
we shall pursue our course without interruption, if possible, until
the triumph of our ideals.

> From *El Socialista*, 14 January 1936, quoted in Burnett
> Bolloten, *The Spanish Revolution* (Chapel Hill, University of
> North Carolina Press, 1979) p 25

Questions

★ *a* What do you understand by the 'Comintern' (line 6) and the
'Popular Front' (line 7)? Why had this strategy been adopted by
the Comintern in 1935?

    b What does extract *a* reveal of Franco's character and methods?

    c What did Franco mean by his statement, 'If you hear of me
going to Africa . . . ' (line 16)?

    d To what extent do the views in extract *b* substantiate the fears of
Franco expressed in extract *a*?

    e What does extract *b* reveal of the relationship between the
Socialists and their allies in the Popular Front?

II The Conspiracy and Military Rising, February to July 1936

Introduction

The Popular Front victory of February 1936 put the Left Republicans in power but with a programme of reforms which the right considered verged on Bolshevism. Their fears were illustrated by the replacement of President Zamora by the anti-clerical Azana in April and particularly by the apparent failure of the government to preserve law and order. 'How serious the breakdown of public order was can never be settled' (R. Carr), but the first few months of 1936 certainly witnessed a 'descent into violence'.

Responsibility for the outbreak of the Civil War has been much debated. It has been blamed on a combination of the 'refusal of the Socialists to join the Popular Front Government and the reaction of the right to its own electoral failure' (R. Carr), or on an 'inevitable clash of extremes'. Stanley Payne considers that the main responsibility rested on the middle class Left Republican government which used its authority to attack the right and 'catered to the Revolutionaries in almost every way'. What is certain is that 'while the left were making revolutionary noises the right were planning counter-revolution'.

The rebellion had been planned from February 1936 though Franco (who had been demoted to the position of Governor of the Canary Islands in March), was at first cautious. It was the assassination of the monarchist politician Calvo Sotelo on 13 July which removed any lingering doubts and hastened the final preparations. The role of the army in the rebellion has been much disputed. In spite of the prominence of Franco and Mola the impetus for the conspiracy came not from the generals so much as from a minority of junior officers organised in the UME (Union Militar Espanola), and the Spanish armed forces on the mainland were evenly divided. The Falange, and the Carlists (the CEDA had declined after its failure in the elections), were included in the plot but until the last moment it proved difficult to win the support of such politically disparate organisations. For this reason the initial aims of the conspirators sometimes appeared contradictory (as seen in the extracts from their manifestos), and they seemed to have no common goal other than the overthrow of Azana's administration.

The rebellion began in Morocco on 17 July and Franco flew to Tetuan to take command of the Army of Africa. Historians have often speculated on why the Republic failed to curb or to deal effectively with a revolt of which it had had prior warning, but in any event the Rising was only partially successful and the rebels failed to capture the great cities of Madrid, Valencia or Barcelona. A decisive factor in determining success or failure is considered to have been the loyalty or otherwise, of the Civil Guards and Assault Guards who were almost as numerous as the Army though it has been claimed also that the 'armed people' played a key role. Paul Preston suggests that if the Government had immediately issued guns to the workers the rising might have been crushed at birth, though Ramon Larrazabel considers that 'the militia, poorly armed and lacking organisation and training were never more than an active chorus'.

At the end of July the advantage seemed to lie with the government which controlled two-thirds of Spain with most of the large cities and industrial resources. But the Army of Africa would sway the balance provided that it could be transported across the Straits. Foreign assistance to Franco was to turn an 'audacious coup' into a prolonged Civil War.

1 The February 1936 elections

(a) Communist Party election poster (see page 22)

(b) The programme of the right

The fortune of Spain, 300,000 million pesetas, will be nationalized and taken over or destroyed by Soviet communism. Those who haven't lost their lives will be out of work – in the street with only the clothes on their backs.
5   Workers, employees, civil servants: if you vote for the communist-socialist-leftist revolutionary bloc, you will be slaves, working only for bad food and poor clothing.
Spaniards: if you have an ounce of sense, an atom of self-preservation, vote with iron discipline for the candidates of the
10   anti-revolutionary front! For the salvation of Spain.
Monarchist paper, *La Nacion*, 15 February 1936, quoted in Fraser, *Blood of Spain,* p 81

(a) Communist Party election poster

(c) The election results

Popular Front

Republican left	117		
Socialists	90		
Esquerra	38		
15 Communists	16		
POUM	1		
Others	9	Total	271

Centre	40		

Right

20 CEDA	86		
Lliga	13		
Carlists	8		
Others	36	Total	143

Stanley Payne, *The Spanish Revolution* (London, Weidenfeld & Nicholson, 1970), p 190

Questions

a Identify the figures depicted in the poster in extract *a*. What view of the Communist Party and of its relations with other parties is given in this poster?

b How persuasively does extract *b* seek to appeal to all classes of Spanish voters?

c Identify the Esquerra (line 14); the Lliga (line 21); the POUM (line 16); and the Carlists (line 22).

★ d Explain the success of the Popular Front in the February 1936 elections.

e What indication do the election results give of the political difficulties facing a Popular Front government?

2 The crisis in the Republic, February – July 1936

(a) Republican reforms

In itself the Popular Front programme could not have been more moderate. . . . With the exception of the amnesty for the victims of the 'two black years', the other points in the Government programme could be summed up as a desire to re-establish the
5 Republic. This involved respect for the constitution and a continuation of the agrarian reform begun in 1931. This agrarian reform by no means implied the nationalisation of lands; on the contrary it was governed by the principle of indemnifying the proprietors whose large uncultivated estates, not only condemned

10 the peasants to a life of misery but also hindered the normal development of the Spanish economy.

        J. Alvarez del Vayo, *Freedom's Battle* (London, Heinemann, 1940), pp 14–15

(b) An interview with the Prime Minister Azana on 4 April 1936

'Why don't you purge the army?'

'Why?' he asked, feigning innocence.

I said, 'some of the generals are opposed to your government.'

15 'No', Azana assured me, 'they are all my friends.'

'A few nights ago there were tanks on the streets and you were in the Ministry of the Interior on the Puerta del Sol until two in the morning. You must have feared a revolt.'

He denied it and attributed his presence there to another reason.

20 I told him I had heard stories of impending trouble by army generals.

'That is cafe gossip', he laughed.

I said I had heard it in the Cortes.

'Ah,' Azana declared, 'that's a big cafe. Besides', he added as an

25 afterthought and with a smile, 'if it were true I wouldn't admit it to you.'

        L. Fischer, *Men and Politics* (London, Cape, 1941), p 307

(c) Calvo Sotelo's speech in the Cortes, 16 June 1936

No more strikes, no more lock-outs, no more usurious interest, no more of capitalism's abusive financial formulae, no more starvation wages, no more political salaries gained by happy accident, no

30 more anarchic liberty, no more criminal loss of production, for national production is above all classes, all parties and all interests.

    Many call that the fascist state. If it is, then I who share that idea of the integrative state and believe in it, declare myself fascist.

        Calvo Sotelo, speech in the Cortes 16 June 1936, quoted in Fraser, *Blood of Spain*, p 91

(d) The assassination of Calvo Sotelo

On 13 July gunmen in a touring car nosed slowly through sparse

35 traffic under the arc lamps of a Madrid street and opened fire with a machine gun at the defenceless back of a man standing chatting on his doorstep and roared off among the tramlines, leaving him dying in a puddle of his own blood on the pavement. . . . That in a manner of speaking was the Sarajevo of the Spanish War. The

40 young man they killed was Jose Castillo, lieutenant of Assault Guards. . . . He was a gallant and patriotic young officer, as dauntless a defender of the Republic as you could wish to see.

Some time before midnight on the night Castillo was shot the storm guards of his troops had already decided to carry out
45 immediately and without waiting for action from above, the arrest of Calvo Sotelo . . . the 'man behind the gun'. In the early hours of the morning a police car under the command of a Lieutenant Moreno drove out to Sotelo's house, got him out of bed and told him he was under arrest. Cornered but still hopeful that the Sotelo
50 money could 'fix' one crime more, Sotelo tried to telephone to friends at government offices. The assault guards, friends of Castillo were impatient. . . . They put him in the police car. . . .

Of what happened next I have heard several conflicting versions, one from a man who was actually in the car at the time. He stated
55 that another car, moving fast without lights, was heard roaring behind them, that they prepared for action against an attempt at armed release of the prisoner and that at the last moment a young assault guard losing his head put a bullet through the back of the subtle politician's head.

> Frank Pitcairn (Claud Cockburn), *Reporter in Spain* (London, Lawrence & Wishart, 1938), pp 16–19

Questions

a   What is meant by 'the two black years' (line 3)? Explain the phrase 'the Sarajevo of the Spanish war' (line 39).

b   What evidence is there in extract *b* to support the view that the Republican government responded to the threat of a military rising with 'irresponsible optimism' (Carr)?

c   What did Calvo Sotelo appear to understand by fascism in his speech in extract *c*?

d   To what extent does Calvo Sotelo's speech in extract *c* explain the events in extract *d*?

e   In what ways does extract *d* reveal the political views of its author and his opinion of Calvo Sotelo?

f   What reservations might a historian have about the account of Calvo Sotelo's death presented in extract *d*? What other sources would you need to consult to arrive at an accurate account of his death?

g   How far could these extracts be used both to support and disprove the view that law and order had broken down in Spain in the spring and summer of 1936?

★   h   The Nationalists claimed that they rebelled in order to prevent a Communist coup in Spain. Is there any evidence that such a coup was likely in July 1936?

★   i   At what point in the 1930s did it begin to seem that Spain could not avoid civil war?

3 The organisation of the rising

(a) Jose Antonio's instructions to the Falange

All territorial and provincial leaders are advised of the circumstances under which they may contract alliances in the event of an
imminent uprising against the present government.

(1) Every territorial and provincial leader must deal *exclusively*
5   with the man actually in charge of the militia movement in that
territory or province and with no-one else.
(2) The Falange will participate in the movement by contributing
its own units with their own commands and their own distinctive
insignia (shirts, emblems and banners).
10   (4) The military leaders must promise the leaders of the Falange
that civil authority will not be transferred to anyone for at least 3
days after the successful completion of the movement and that
during that time civil authority will remain in the hands of the
military.

> Orders of Jose Antonio Primo de Rivera, 29 June 1936,
> smuggled out of Alicante prison, quoted in Thomas (ed.),
> *Jose Antonio Primo de Rivera, Selected Writings,* pp 258–9

(b) An English publisher describes the planning of Franco's flight to Morocco

15   It was in July when Luis Bolin [the London correspondent of the
monarchist paper ABC], rang up and asked me to lunch. I looked
at my engagements and suggested a day next week. 'No, no, I'm
afraid it must be today. It's important,' . . . We lunched at
Simpsons and de le Cierva completed the party. We began with
20   appropriate gestures of conspiracy. We must have a quiet table. By
the time Bolin and de la Cierva after much whispering had rejected
every vacant table in the room hardly anyone could have been
unaware of our pressing need for privacy. We wanted to be quite
alone.
25   We had begun to eat and as the atmosphere then was less electric
I thought it would be safe to broach the subject of our meeting.
And then it happened. 'I want a man and three platinum blondes to
fly to Africa tomorrow.' 'Must there really be three?' I asked and at
that Bolin turned triumphantly to de la Cierva, 'I told you he
30   would manage it!' 'Well probably two would be enough,' Bolin
said regretfully . . . 'but of course the man must have had some
experience; there might be trouble.'
After all the job was Pollard's by rights for he had experience of
Moroccan, Mexican and Irish revolutions and of course this meant
35   war, and he knew Spain. I telephoned him and asked, 'Can you fly

to Africa tomorrow with two girls?' and heard the expected reply, 'Depends upon the girls'. 'You can choose' said I in my best business accents. 'I'll bring two Spanish friends down to see you this afternoon.' 'Right' said Pollard 'I'll expect you to tea.' 'There's only one point I ought to mention' I said as Hugh was ringing off, 'the aeroplane may be stolen when you get there. In that case you come back by boat.' 'First class?' 'Why not?' 'Right, can do, goodbye.'

That might have seemed the hardest part of my job but there was still the business of getting to Pollard to be solved. Train was impossible and no-one knew the way to Fernhurst. De la Cierva, the practical man, suggested buying a map and so we finished our lunch and went to Phillips in the Strand. We bought our map of Sussex easily and as we were leaving Bolin said, 'Let's get a map of Spain and North Africa. It might be useful.' It was. The next time I saw that map it was in Franco's HQ in Salamanca.

Then to Fernhurst. . . . When I saw Pollard I took him on one side and explained to him with an assurance that I could not possibly have justified that his aeroplane, containing three self-styled English tourists, would be stolen if the anticipated crisis arose, at the Canaries to take General Franco to Morocco. Round the table we got down to business. Passports, money, the route to Casablanca. Afterwards, anything might happen. 'Pack a gun?' And again de la Cierva laughed and said, 'this is incredible'.

Then began the most arduous search of all. Pollard's daughter was to be one of the party but the other girl was out, no telephone inquiries could locate her. All that was known was that she was delivering chickens somewhere and that she hadn't got a passport. And so the last crusade began on a hot July afternoon with four men searching frantically up and down Sussex lanes for a girl delivering chickens and who had not got a passport. In despair we turned into the pub and there, the heavens being kind and the bar being open, we found her. 'Dorothy, come here. You're going to Africa tomorrow,' Hugh shouted cheerfully. 'Africa where's that? Who does it belong to?' 'Oh you know, it used to belong to Cecil Rhodes and now it belongs to Mussolini.' 'Oh that place!' 'Well that's settled.' I suddenly realised that I was going to be very late for dinner and so we went home.

Ten days later General Franco, supposed to be safely relegated to the Canaries, raised his standard in Morocco. Arriba Espana! Luis Bolin was in Rome and Hugh Pollard from the window of his bedroom in an hotel in Palmas heard the volley of musketry which began and ended the revolution there. And Dorothy was fast asleep!

D. Jerrold, *Georgian Adventure* (London, Collins, 1937), pp 369–73

(c) An account by the pilot of the Dragon Rapide

80　On the afternoon of 9 July a Spaniard walked into our office at
Croydon aerodrome and asked to see Captain Olley of Olley Air
Services. Ten minutes later I was called into the office and asked if I
would undertake a secret flight to the Canary Islands, the
stipulation being that I was not allowed to fly over or land in
85　Spain. . . .

　　We started at dawn on 11 July and I had on board one
Englishman, his daughter and another girl and a Spaniard. . . . On
the 15 July we left Casablanca for Las Palmas arriving at 2.00
pm. . . . [On the 18th] I was rushed to the aerodrome with an
90　armed escort in half a dozen cars. At half past one a tug was
sighted. Engines were started. I now realised for certain that my
passenger was General Franco the leader of the insurgent movement . . . the most dramatic meeting of my life was the meeting
with General Franco. . . . I saw the tug come in and a man in
95　general's uniform climb out over the side into a rowing boat
accompanied by an armed escort of six. . . . He stood before me, a
smart military figure, smiling, the essence of coolness. . . . While
we were flying over the South Atlantic he changed out of his
uniform and threw his passport and all other documents of
100　identification out of the windows. Eventually we landed at Agadir
at 5.00 pm. After refuelling we took off again for Casablanca where
we landed at 9.00 pm. We were smuggled from the aerodrome into
a guest house outside the town and started off for Tetuan in Spanish
Morocco at 8.00 pm the following morning.

105　　As we landed in Tetuan the foreign legions of the Spanish army
were there to welcome us. When we touched down General Franco
was given a royal welcome. As he stepped out a mighty cheer
echoed over the flying field.

　　　　Article by Captain Bebb in the *News Chronicle*, 7 November
　　　　1936

Questions

★　*a*　Why did Jose Antonio order his followers to observe the
stipulations in extract *a*?

★　*b*　Explain the references to 'the last crusade' (line 64); 'Cecil
Rhodes' (lines 70–1); and 'Mussolini' (line 71)

★　*c*　Why had Franco been 'relegated to the Canaries' and why was
his flight to Spanish Morocco vital for the success of the plot?

　　d　Why did Franco 'change out of his uniform . . .' during the
flight and why did the party from the Dragon Rapide have to be
'smuggled from the aeroplane to a guest house' in Casablanca
(extract *c*)?

★　*e*　Using extracts *b* and *c* and other sources construct a chronology
of the movements of the Dragon Rapide from 11 to 19 July.

　　f　What does the article by Captain Bebb reveal of the author's
views of Franco?

4 The aims of the insurgents

(a) Franco's manifesto

Spaniards! To whomsoever feels a sacred love for Spain; to those of you, who in the ranks of the Army and Navy have made a profession of your faith in the service of the Mother Country; to those of you who swore to resist your enemies even unto death; the
5 nation calls to her defence.

The situation in Spain is becoming more critical with every day that passes; anarchy reigns in most of her villages and fields; government-appointed authorities preside over the revolts, when they are not actually fomenting them. Differences are settled by
10 pistol-shots and with machine-guns among the mobs of townspeople, who traitorously and treacherously kill each other, without the public authorities imposing peace and justice. Revolutionary strikes of all kinds are paralysing the life of the nation, dissipating and destroying its sources of wealth, and creating a state of hunger
15 that will drive working men to desperation. To the revolutionary and unheeding spirit of the masses hoaxed and exploited by the Soviet agents who veil the bloody reality of that regime . . . are joined the maliciousness and negligence of authorities of all kinds. . . .
20 Can we abandon Spain to the enemies of the Mother Country, handing her over without a struggle and without resistance, by our cowardly and traitorous behaviour? Justice and Equality before the law we offer you; peace and love between Spaniards . . . work for all. Social justice, accomplished without rancour or violence, and
25 an equitable and progressive distribution of wealth without destroying or jeopardizing the Spanish economy.
Spaniards: Long live Spain!!!
Long live the honourable Spanish people!!!

> Manifesto of Las Palmas, 18 July 1936, quoted in B. Crozier, *Franco* (London, Eyre & Spottiswoode, 1967) pp 519–22

(b) A monarchist manifesto

We are fighting totally for Spain and for civilisation. Nor are we
30 fighting alone; twenty centuries of Western Civilisation lie behind us. We are fighting for God, for our land and our dead. . . . It has always been Spain's providential and historic mission to save the civilised world from all dangers; expelling moors. stopping turks, baptizing indians. . . . Now new turks, red and cruel asiatics, are
35 again threatening Europe. But Spain today as yesterday, opposes them, saves and redeems civilisation. Because this is a holy war, a crusade of civilisation. . . .

> Broadcast over Seville radio, 15 August 1936, quoted in H. Browne, *Spain's Civil War* (London, Longman, 1983), pp 83–4

(c) Jose Antonio's manifesto

A group of Spaniards, some of them soldiers and other civilians, is
unwilling to stand by and watch the total disintegration of the
40   fatherland. These men rise up today against a government that is
treacherous, incompetent, cruel and unjust and which is about to
lead our country to its ruin. . . . The army, the fleet, the police are
undermined by agents of Moscow, sworn enemies of Spanish
civilisation. . . . The abject ferocity of their latest deed [the murder
45   of Calvo Sotelo] has no parallel in modern Europe and may be
equated with the most sombre pages of the Russian Cheka. . . .

Paths of splendour are opening up before Spain, this ancient land
of ours with its missionary and military zeal, its rustic and seafaring
virtues. . . . Our victory will not be that of a reactionary clique
50   and the people will not lose any advantage thereby. On the
contrary ours will be a national effort which will succeed in raising
the people's standard of living, truly horrific at present in some
parts of the country, and which will enable them all to share in the
pride of a great destiny regained.
55   Workers, farmers, intellectuals, soldiers, sailors, guardians of the
fatherland: shake off your despair at the sight of its collapse and join
us on the route towards a Spain that is one great and free! May God
be with us! Arriba Espana!

> Thomas (ed.), *Jose Antonio Primo de Rivera, Selected Writings,*
> pp 262–4

Questions

a   Explain the statement 'expelling moors, stoping turks, baptis-
ing indians' (lines 33–4).

b   Explain the references to 'new turks, red and cruel asiatics' (line
34); and 'the Russian Cheka' (line 46).

c   To what extent do extracts *b* and *c* provide a similar explanation
for the rising to that offered in Franco's manifesto in extract *a*?

d   Which of the manifestos makes the greatest appeal for support
from the poorer classes in Spain? Give reasons for your choice.

★   *e*   How accurate a picture of life in Spain under the Popular Front
government is portrayed in extracts *a* and *c*?

f   How far can these extracts be used to substantiate the view that
the organisers of the rising sought to revive Spain's imperial
past rather than to constuct a new state?

5 The rising: success and failure

(a) Pamplona

Wearing their red Carlist berets, the people streamed towards the
Plaza del Castillo. At the entrance to the town the guardia civil had

stopped the car and Dolores Baleztena's nineteen year old nephew, rather cautiously had pulled out his red beret. 'Forward . . . ' At
5 last – the red beret was a passport.

As she drove into the square, tears came to Baleztena's eyes. Recognising her, sister of the president of the Navarre regional Carlist junta, people stretched out their hands. She let go the steering wheel to grasp the hands. People were shouting, 'Long live
10 Religion! Long live the King! Long live brave Navarre!' The people seemed delirious.

Shouts of joy, happy faces. The population was sweeping in off the land. Lorries, tractors, farm carts bringing red berets from every side street into the square. Most of the people in their Sunday
15 best. A man in shirt-sleeves leapt from a lorry crying: 'Here we've come, confessed and communed, for whatever God demands.' . . . These were the real, authentic people determined to defend their ideals. The people who loved their land, their farms, who had a pride in their race, even if pride was no virtue.
20 In the Plaza del Castillo, the requetes were ordered to form up. The red and gold flag which the republic had done away with was hoisted on the provincial government building and the town hall to the frantic cheers of the crowds; and soon afterwards was ordered removed by General Mola. . . .
25 General Mola had reviewed the column of troops, requetes and falangists. 'Ala lads we're going to save Spain,' Antonio Izu, peasant requete, heard him say as he passed down the ranks smiling with his hands in the air . . . then [recalled Rafael Garcia Serrano, a falangist volunteer], he told us we were setting out for Madrid.
30 That had always been the idea of the falangists – the decisive moment. We were much influenced by Mussolini's March on Rome.

Fraser, *Blood of Spain*, pp 64–5 & 70, eyewitness accounts of events in Pamplona on 19 July

(b) The rising in Burgos

Suddenly on the morning of the 17 July came the astounding news that the Army in Africa was in revolt, that the rebellion had been
35 initiated by the Foreign Legion under Yague and that all the forces in Morocco were following his lead.

The people of Burgos discussed the news joyfully, making no secret of their sympathies. . . .

The whole affair appeared to be much more serious than I had
40 thought. I paid a visit to the Governor, a gallant but unfortunate gentleman who was extremely ingenuous and over-confident – the classic type of Republican Governor. What he said somewhat allayed my fears. 'It's nothing,' he told me, 'just a mad scheme of

Yague's – purely local, with no response anywhere in the
45   peninsula, with no ramifications whatever here.' 'But surely', I
ventured to say, 'things are very unsettled here. The garrison . . . '
      'No, no, there's no need to be alarmed. Why the City Council
have just assured me of their support. I've also had very friendly
visits from the leading officers of the Civil Guard and of the Army
50   who were all most cordial.' . . .
      Night came and the atmosphere could not have been more
ominous. I went back to my hotel early that evening and passed on
the way several groups of workers peacefully walking along to the
headquarters of their organisations. . . .
55   I was about to fall into a sleep of nervous exhaustion when I was
roused by an urgent telephone call. There was to be a meeting of all
civil authorities and I was ordered to attend. I hurried along to the
Town Hall. . . . In the civil Governor's suite the chief officers of
the garrison with few exceptions, as well as the civil authorities
60   who had been summoned were assembled. General Davila,
Lieutenant Colonel Gavilan and Major Pastran appeared to be in
charge. . . .
      The local military commander had declared martial law on the
strength of a proclamation by Mola who had assumed supreme
65   authority in that region. . . .
      Lieutenant Colonel Gavilan addressed the meeting. 'Gentlemen',
he said, 'this is a serious moment and calls for a clear stand. I trust I
can rely on all of you to support this military movement.'
      All those present gave their assent; then the Mayor, a prominent
70   member of the Conservative Republican Party made a protest.
      'I feel I should tell you gentlemen that I am, always have been
and always shall be, a Republican.'
      'We're not dealing with that now', rapped out Gavilan, 'it isn't a
question of Monarchy or Republic. Our business is to turn out the
75   Popular Front Government which came in at the elections. There'll
be plenty of time later on to settle the other matter.'
      'In that case', said the Mayor, 'you can count entirely on
me.' . . .
      Orders were given and duly carried out for the arrest of large
80   numbers of people . . . and when at last day dawned on that
unforgettable 18 July, all the officers of the new regime went to the
church nearby to hear Mass and receive the episcopal blessing.
      The city was soon bedecked with flags and banners, many of
them, although not yet all, being the monarchial colours. . . .
85   In my brief account of what happened in Burgos at the outbreak
of the military rebellion the reader will have noticed something that
may seem surprising – that I make no mention whatever of
Phalangists or Fascists. This omission of any reference to the Blue
shirts is easily explained if one bears in mind that at Burgos as in

90   most of the cities where there was a rising, there were no fascists to speak of.

A.R. Vilaplana (a lawyer working for the Burgos local government), *Burgos Justice* (Constable, London, 1938) pp 17–26

(c) Events in Barcelona

That night [17 July] 10,000 men stood on the Rambla demanding arms. CNT leaders demanded arms from the Generalidad. Companys hesitated. . . . A group of men went down to the harbour,
95   'found' arms on a boat, those originally destined for the transport strike. With 150 rifles they enforced their demands. A limited number of rifles were issued. . . . At midday [on 18 July] the unions broadcast to their members instructions, – all organised workers were asked to come immediately to their union centres
100   with arms if possible. . . .

    Saturday afternoon was outwardly calm but the sun-beaten streets were strangely empty. As it grew dark the usual Rambla paseo was unusually animated. . . . In the union centres the volunteers patrols were organising. There were not nearly enough
105   arms. The shock police seemed loyal but the civil guard, as always, was an unknown factor and there were strange tales from the barracks up in the north of the city. . . . Doubts about the loyalty of the civil guard were set at rest when a section of the 19th division . . . appeared on the Ramblas late in the evening. The crowd
110   applauded them and after a moment's hesitation they raised their fists in the Popular Front salute. . . .

    At 5 o'clock [on 19 July] the first shots disturbed Barcelona's uneasy sleep . . . the regiments from the barracks in the north had begun to move down onto the centre of the city. At the other end
115   of the town down by the docks, the rebels held the Atarazanas barracks. Generals Goded and Burriel and Captain Lopez Varela were in command. If the troops marching from the north could cross the central square, the Plaza Calatuna and make the junction with Alarazana at the other end of the Ramblas, the main part of the
120   city would be cut in two and the two semi-circles would be reduced by other columns moving round their perimeter, the Rondas. . . . The first columns had exchanged shots with a few police patrols who retired before overwhelming odds, but when the troops arrived at the outer circles of the inner city the Calle
125   Cortes . . . resistance was intense. At first the action was sustained by the shock police and loyal civil guards supported by a few militia patrols but soon the whole population of Barcelona joined in. . . . The battle began furiously. Now the militia were in action. The militia, men, women and children fought like furies. . . .

130 It was now perfectly clear that this was an officers' putsch
. . . the soldiers realising how they had been deceived, fraternised
with the workers wherever they could. They brought much needed
arms and were welcomed with frantic enthusiasm. . . . The
insurrection was lost as soon as the soldiers fraternised and the
135 militia had arms. Outside the Capitania where Goded and his
officers had barricaded themselves, the guns roared against the
building, smashing splinters off the facade. All Sunday the fighting
went on. . . . At dawn [20 July] the firing began again . . . the
Capitania was taken by storm after bombardment. . . . Goded was
140 removed in a police car. Few of the other officers survived
. . . . The battle of Barcelona was over by Monday evening.
  Jellinek, *Civil War in Spain*, pp 268–324.

(d) Madrid

The Government on 18 July gave an order to arm the people.
Minutes later police wagons loaded with heavy boxes were racing
through the streets to the trade union and political HQs where
145 anxious crowds stood wondering whether they were to survive or
be crushed. . . .

 In Madrid the officers simply could not make up their minds to
take the plunge . . . a man whom I knew and who was doing his
military service in a Madrid barracks described to me afterwards
150 how the officers in their quarters argued furiously hour after hour
as to whether they should rebel or not. General Fanjul waited till
Monday morning [20 July] before he showed signs of rebellion.
. . . On Monday morning I awoke to hear the boom of cannon
. . . . Out on the streets I saw a new Madrid. Overnight, the
155 youths, girls and more mature citizens of the trade unions and
political organisations had apparently adopted a more or less
general uniform of a blue overall. Cars had been requisitioned.
Groups of workers drove fast and furiously around the town
having the time of their lives. . . . The district I was in was so full
160 of minor battles that my progress was slow when I set out from
home.

 The main battle fought in Madrid, the taking of the Montana
barracks, had been over for some time when I reached the scene.
General Fanjul had shut himself up in the barracks on Saturday.
165 . . . A picturesque but determined motley of police, soldiers,
workers, lookers-on assaulted the barracks furiously with the aid of
some ancient artillery and some light bombs dropped from
aeroplanes. In four or five hours the battle was over. The mob
rushed the gate. About 160 Fascists who were caught, were shot in
170 the courtyard.

  Buckley, *Life and Death of the Spanish Republic,* p 211

Questions

★ *a*   Explain the reference to Mussolini's march on Rome, (lines 31–2). Why were the falangists much influenced by it?

    b   What was meant in the context of the extract by: 'a junta' (line 8), 'the King' (line 10); 'requetes' (line 27); 'Blue shirts' (line 89); 'generalidad' (line 93); 'shock police' (line 105); 'militia patrols' (line 127)?

    c   According to extracts *a* and *b* what institutions and individuals supported the rising in Pamplona and Burgos?

★ *d*   Why did Mola order the red and gold flag to be removed (extract *a*)?

    e   What evidence is there in extract *b* to indicate that the authorities in Burgos were unprepared for the rising?

    f   What do extracts *a* and *b* reveal of the different aims of those involved in the rising?

    g   According to extracts *a* and *b* how important was the role of the Falange in the Rising?

    h   Why do you think the authorities in Barcelona and Madrid were reluctant to issue arms to the populace?

    i   'The loyalty of the Civil Guards and the Assault Guards in towns where the Republic maintained its hold was certainly as decisive as proletarian action' (Carr). Comment on this statement in the light of the material in extracts *c* and *d*.

★ *j*   Why did only part of the Spanish army support the rising?

6   Republican and Nationalist Spain in August 1936

(a) *Map of the division of Spain in August 1936* (see page 36)

(b) *Republican and Nationalist advantages*

In appraising the prospects of success of the opposing sides the following should be taken into account:

    A. The Government has the advantage of the inner line, possession of the Central Government machinery with unified
5   leadership and with the banks of issue and the gold reserves of the Bank of Spain. In the Guardia Civil it possesses the best troops in Spain, in addition to the Guardia de Asalto and the Red Militias; the latter while of little military value is filled with fanatics. Disadvantageous for the Government are the comparative barrenness and
10   lack of depth of the strip of land it controls, which can lead to shortages of food and war material if the fight lasts for any length of time; in addition the small number of trained officers, since most of these revolted or have already been taken prisoner.

    B The rebels. Their advantage consists in the greater expanse of

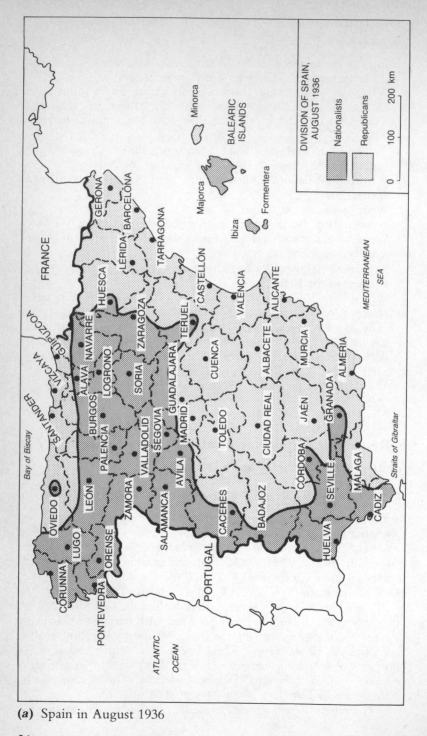

(a) Spain in August 1936

15   the area controlled by them containing the greater part of Spain's
      natural resources and armament industries. Furthermore they have
      on their side the greater part of the regular army, almost the entire
      officer corps, among them a number of capable generals, and
      finally the entire Moroccan army of approximately 40,000 men.
20   Disadvantageous for the rebels are the lack of geographical and
      organisational cohesion and the great distances, but above all the
      opposition of the lower strata of the population in the cities. Lastly
      they lack ideological unity and objectives.

> Documents on German Foreign Policy 1918–45, Series D, Vol 1
> (HMSO, 1949), p 5, German Embassy in Spain to the
> German Foreign Office, 23/7/36

(c) The military balance at the beginning of the war

Army

25   20% of the Divisional Generals, 30% of the Brigadier Generals and
      66% of the junior officers joined the rising.

	Republic	Nationalists
Regular army in peninsula	33,000	23,000
Army of Africa	—	24,000
Civil Guards	20,000	14,000
Assault Guards & armed police	22,000	9,000
	Militias	Carlists requetes & Falangists
Airforce	3,000	2,000
Navy Crews	9,000	2,000
Officers	300	1,300

(Information compiled from secondary sources)

Questions

★   *a*   Why would an assessment of the advantages and disadvantages
          of the Republicans and Nationalists be of interest to the German
          Foreign Office in July 1936?
    b   What can you learn from the map in extract *a* about the
          advantages and disadvantages of the Republicans and National-
          ists in August 1936? What additional information on this subject
          is provided by extract *b*?
    c   How optimistic is the German Ambassador on the Nationalists'
          chances of success in the war?
    d   What evidence is provided by extract *c* to support the view that
          the Army of Africa held the balance in the opening stages of the
          Civil War?
★   *e*   How had the Nationalists improved their military position by
          the end of October 1936?

III International Involvement in the War

Introduction

The war quickly acquired an international dimension. Franco immediately requested aid from Hitler through two Nazi businessmen based in Morocco. Against the inclinations of the German Foreign Office, Hitler decided to send transport planes to airlift the Army of Africa across the Straits and later, in October, sent the Condor Legion, a mixed air and tank unit which was kept up to strength for the duration of the war. Mussolini, mainly in response to representations from Spanish Monarchists, also provided aircraft and by February 1938 had sent more than 50,000 troops to Spain.

After initial hesitation Stalin assisted the Republic with tanks, aircraft and up to 2000 military advisers, obtaining in return the entire Spanish gold reserves, which were shipped to Russia in October 1936. The Republic had first looked for aid to the Popular Front government in France but Blum opted for non-intervention, along with Britain. The Non-intervention Committee established in London in September 1936 ineffectually tried to prevent the flow of arms and volunteers to Spain, in Anthony Eden's words 'a leaking dam but better than no dam at all'. It has also been described as 'institutionalised hypocrisy' since, although it purported to treat both sides equally, it in effect discriminated against the legitimate Spanish government.

The war aroused great passions outside Spain. The Comintern organised the International Brigades of volunteers for the Republic, usually led by foreign Communists exiled in Moscow. These arrived in time to play a significant part in the defence of Madrid in November 1936.

Historians writing on the subject of foreign intervention have been largely concerned with the motives of the various powers. Each responded to events in Spain in the context of their wider foreign policy ambitions. It used to be thought that Hitler's chief motives were economic advantages (as stated by Goering at the Nuremburg Trials), and a training ground for the Luftwaffe, but recent scholarship has revealed that 'his primary purpose was a matter of long-term diplomacy and strategic considerations, to ensure a pro-German government in Madrid which would limit France's political and military options' (H. Browne). A second objective was for Hitler to 'consolidate his already good relations with Mussolini' (R. Whealey), thus paving the way for *Anschluss* with Austria and expansion into central Europe.

Mussolini wished to prevent a Communist Spain but also had more grandiose ambitions to make Italy the centre of a Mediterranean Fascist empire. Hitler was arguably to benefit more from intervention in Spain than Mussolini who incurred military and financial losses with few tangible gains.

Aid to the Republic was part of Stalin's quest for Soviet security against Nazi Germany by the creation of an anti-fascist front in Western Europe. He had to steer a precarious and ultimately unsuccessful course, between preserving the Republic and avoiding antagonising Britain and France. Soviet influence over the Republican governments proved much greater than corresponding German or Italian influence over Franco with consequent effects on the outcome of the war.

The French reasons for adopting non-intervention have been the subject of much historical debate. It used to be thought that 'French willingness to help the Republic was overridden by British pressure', but most historians now consider political divisions in French society and right-wing pressure on Blum's government to have been the most important factor.

Also the subject of argument among historians has been the impact of foreign intervention on the outcome of the war. Certainly the support of Germany and Italy for Franco turned a partly failed coup into a prolonged conflict. Many Republicans chose to ascribe their defeat to German and Italian armaments and to non-intervention. Hugh Thomas identifies a number of points at which it was crucial, for example the German airlift of the Army of Africa saved the rising in its early stages, while Soviet aid made a major contribution to the defence of Madrid in the autumn of 1936. However, the importance of foreign involvement should not be exaggerated. Spaniards always comprised the bulk of the armies in Spain and after the spring of 1938 foreign aid diminished.

1 German aid to the Nationalists

(a) Franco requests aid

General Franco and Lieutenant Colonel Beigbeder send greeting to their friend the hon. General Kuhlental [the German military attache], inform him of the new Nationalist Spanish Government

and request that he send ten troop-transport planes with maximum
5 seating capacity through private German firms. Transfer by air
with German crews to any airfield in Spanish Morocco. The
contract will be signed afterwards. Very urgent! On the word of
General Franco of Spain.

> *Documents on German Foreign Policy, Series D, Vol 1* (HMSO,
> 1949), p 3, note from the German consul at Tetuan to the
> German Foreign Ministry, 22 July 1936

(b) The response of the German Foreign Office

There arrived in Berlin yesterday by Lufthansa plane two officers
10 of the Spanish rebels bringing instructions of General Franco to
negotiate with our authorities for the purchase of planes and war
materials. In my opinion it is absolutely necessary that at this stage
the German Government and Party authorities continue to refrain
from any contact with the two officers. Arms deliveries to the
15 rebels would become known very soon. . . .

> *Documents on German Foreign Policy*, pp 10–11, Memoran-
> dum by the Director of the Political Department, Berlin, 25
> July 1936

(c) Ribbentrop recalls Hitler's decision to send aid

In the early Summer of 1936 an invitation from the Führer to the
Wagner Festival in Bayreuth, arrived. I had never been there and
looked forward to some pleasant days. Alas it was not to be for no
sooner had I arrived in Bayreuth than news arrived of the serious
20 turn of events in Spain. . . .

On the following day I reported to the Führer . . . he was
preoccupied and immediately began to talk about Spain; he told me
that Franco had asked for a number of aircraft to ferry troops from
Africa to Spain. . . . My immediate reaction was that we would do
25 well to keep out of Spanish affairs. No laurels were to be won there
and in my view Spain was too dangerous to touch. I feared fresh
complications with Britain which undoubtedly would dislike
German intervention. But Hitler persisted in his opinion and
explained, again proving how much his thoughts were influenced
30 by ideology, – that Germany would in no circumstances tolerate a
communist Spain . . . he had already ordered that aircraft be put at
Franco's disposal. Adolf Hitler rejected my frequent pleas, declaring that, what was, in the last analysis, at issue in the Spanish Civil
War was whether the Soviets would be able to establish a firm grip
35 on a Western country. . . .

The Führer said 'if Spain really goes Communist, France in her
present situation will also be bolshevised in due course and then
Germany is finished. Wedged between the powerful Soviet bloc in

the East and a strong Communist French-Spanish bloc in the West
40 we could do hardly anything if Moscow chose to attack us.'

> *The Ribbentrop Memoirs* (London, Weidenfeld & Nicolson,
> 1954), pp 59–60. (These were written by Ribbentrop in
> prison after the war in August–September 1945)

Questions

★ *a* Why did Franco describe his request for aid as 'very urgent'
       (line 7)?
   b What reasons for refusing aid are stated or implied in extracts *b*
       and *c*?
   c Judging from extract *c* what appear to have been Hitler's main
       motives in aiding the Nationalists?
★ *d* How surprising do you find Hitler's statement in the last line of
       extract *c*?
   e How reliable as evidence for the historian are the recollections
       of Ribbentrop in extract *c*?
★ *f* The Spanish Civil War has been described as a 'sideshow' in
       Hitler's foreign policy. How true do you think this description
       is?

2 Italian aid to the Nationalists

(a) Franco sends Louis Bolin to obtain aid from Mussolini

[on 19 July in Tetuan] I pointed out [to Franco] that it looked as if
we were short of planes. 'Where can we get them?' asked the
General. 'The French must be ruled out,' I said. . . . 'In Germany I
don't think I would be much use, I can't speak the language. But I
5   could make myself useful in Italy. Shall I go there?' It was decided
that I should fly to Italy with a stop in Lisbon to see General
Sanjurjo and inform him of Franco's arrival in Tetuan. . . .

It was mid-afternoon when I arrived in Rome [21 July]. I drove
to the Grand Hotel and was shown to a spacious room where I
10 unpacked and had a bath. . . . A long distance phone call arrived
from King Alfonso [in Austria] . . . the more I said, the more he
pressured me for news and his interest was vehement and
insatiable. Finally he announced that the Marques de Viana, a close
friend of his, had left to help me in Italy. Viana arrived the next
15 morning. . . . Thanks to an influential friend, in a matter of hours
he arranged a meeting with Count Ciano, the Italian Minister for
Foreign Affairs. . . .

Ciano received us in his sumptuous office. Without hesitating an
instant he promised us the necessary aid. 'We must put an end to
20 the Communist threat in the Mediterranean,' he cried. Suddenly he
pulled himself up, 'You realise of course,' he said, 'that I must

speak to a certain person before giving you a definite answer?'

The next day we were met by Signor Anfuso the Foreign
Minister's Chef de Cabinet. . . . His Excellency had considered
25 our proposals. Deeply as he regretted this he found it impossible to
accept them. . . .

[A few days later] Ciano received us with a smile. [By this time
Mola had sent the Monarchist leader Goicoechea who had
negotiated with Mussolini in 1934, to Rome] 'Everything is
30 settled,' he told us. 'My Consul in Tangier has seen General
Franco. We are sending you bombers and fighters. In due course
we may send more.'

L. Bolin, *Spain the Vital Years* (London, Cassell, 1967), pp
52, 167–70

(b) Mussolini explains Italian aims in Spain in November 1937

First of all we have spent about four and a half milliards in Spain.
. . . German expenditure according to what Goering said is in the
35 region of three and a half milliards. We wish to be paid and must be
paid. But there is also over and above that a political aspect. We
want Nationalist Spain which has been saved by virtue of all
manner of Italian and German aid to remain closely associated with
our manoeuvres. . . . Rome and Berlin must therefore keep in
40 close contact so as to act in such a way that Franco will always
follow our policy. . . .

Ribbentrop would like to know our exact position in Majorca
and what agreements there are concerning it.

The Duce replies that . . . it is a fact that we have established at
45 Palma a naval and air base; we keep ships permanently stationed
there and have three airfields. We intend to remain in that situation
as long as possible. In any case Franco must come to understand
that, even after our eventual evacuation, Majorca must remain an
Italian base in the event of a war with France.

M. Muggeridge (ed.), *Ciano's Diplomatic Papers* (London,
Odhams, 1948), p 144

(c) The German Ambassador in Rome reviews German and Italian policy towards Spain in December 1936

50 The interests of Germany and Italy in the Spanish troubles coincide
to the extent that both countries are seeking to prevent a victory for
Bolshevism in Spain. . . . However, while Germany is not pur-
suing any immediate diplomatic interests in Spain beyond this, the
efforts of Rome undoubtedly extend towards having Spain fall in
55 line with its Mediterranean policy, or at least toward preventing
political co-operation between Spain on the one hand and France

and/or England on the other. . . . In connection with the general
policy indicated above, Germany has in my opinion every reason
for being gratified if Italy continues to interest herself deeply in the
60   Spanish affair. . . . The struggle for dominant political influence in
Spain lays bare the natural opposition between Italy and France; at
the same time the position of Italy as a power in the western
Mediterranean comes into competition with that of Britain. All the
more clearly will Italy recognise the advisability of confronting the
65   Western powers shoulder to shoulder with Germany. . . . In my
opinion the guiding principle for us arising out of this situation is
that we should let Italy take the lead in her Spanish policy. . . . We
surely have no reason for jealousy if Fascism takes the fore in the
thorny task of creating a political and social content behind the
70   hitherto purely military and negatively anti-Red label. . . .
    We must deem it desirable if there is created south of France a
factor which, freed from Bolshevism and removed from the
hegemony of the Western powers but on the other hand allied with
Italy, makes the French and British stop to think – a factor
75   opposing the transit of French troops from Africa and one which in
the economic field takes our needs fully into consideration.
        Documents on German Foreign Policy, pp 170–3, Report of the
        German Ambassador in Rome to the German Foreign
        Ministry, 18 December 1936.

Questions

   a Identify Ribbentrop (line 42).
★ *b* Who was Sanjurjo (line 7)? Why was it considered necessary for
      Bolin to inform him of Franco's arrival in Tetuan?
★ *c* Why did King Alfonso display 'vehement and insatiable'
      interest in the fate of the rising (lines 12–13)?
   d Who was the 'certain person' referred to in line 22 and why did
      Ciano have to defer to his opinion?
★ *e* Why did Bolin consider that 'the French must be ruled out' (line
      3)?
   f What light do extracts *a*, *b* and *c* throw on Italian motives for
      intervention in Spain?
   g In what ways does extract *c* suggest that Germany was likely to
      benefit more than Italy from intervention in Spain?
   h Why did the German Ambassador consider that Italy would
      find it advisable to confront the Western powers 'shoulder to
      shoulder with Germany' (line 65)?
★ *i* How and when did Germany and Italy eventually come to
      'stand shoulder to shoulder' against the Western powers?

3 France, Britain and Non-intervention

(a) Sir Samuel Hoare advocates non-intervention

When I speak of 'neutrality' I mean strict neutrality, that is to say, a situation in which the Russians neither officially or unofficially give help to the Communists. On no account must we do anything to bolster up Communism in Spain, particularly when it is remem-
5 bered that Communism in Portugal to which it would probably spread and particularly Lisbon would be a grave danger to the British empire.

> Statement at a Cabinet meeting on 3 August 1936, quoted in J. Edwards, *The British Government and the Spanish Civil War 1936–39* (London, Macmillan, 1979), p 23. Hoare was at this time First Lord of the Admiralty.

(b) The Report of the Chiefs of Staff, 24 August 1936

1. Our interests in the present Spanish crisis are the maintenance:
(a) of the territorial integrity of Spain and her possessions; and
10 (b) of such relations with any Spanish Government which may emerge from this conflict as will ensure benevolent neutrality in the event of our being engaged in a European war;
2. Open intervention by Italy in support of the insurgents in Spain would precipitate a major international crisis;
15 4. The Italian occupation of any part of Spanish Morocco, and particulary of Ceuta, would be a threat to vital British interests;
5. The Italian occupation of any of the Balearic Islands, Canary Islands, and/or Rio de Oro, is highly undesirable from the point of view of British interests, but cannot be regarded as a vital menace;
20 6. Any of the contingencies specified above would be injurious in greater or lesser degree to French interests;
7. The conclusion of any Italo-Spanish alliance would constitute a threat to vital British interests.
The Chiefs of Staff recommend that:
25 1. The principle that should govern any action on the part of His Majesty's Government should be that it is most important to avoid any measures which, while failing to achieve our object, merely tend further to alienate Italy;
3. If no general agreement can be reached, we should impress on
30 the French the desirability of giving no cause for intervention by Italy.

> Quoted in Edwards, *British Government and the Spanish Civil War,* pp 36–7

(c) The Spanish envoy describes the French government's divisions on Spain, 25 July 1936

Last night on my return from London, I was urgently summoned by the Leader of the Government to his house, where I found the four Ministers, who . . . possess more influence within the Cabi-
35 net, owing to the nature of the departments they direct. . . . At their request I made a few considerations upon the character of the Spanish struggle, which cannot be looked upon as being strictly national owing to a series of reasons which we analysed: military frontier in the Pyrenees, Balearic Isles, Straits of Gibraltar, Canaries
40 and breakage of the political unity of Western Europe.

Duty therefore, and direct interest on the part of France to help us. How? We examined our demands and, from the attitude of the Ministers, I gathered that there existed a divergence of opinions. A new question arose: that Spanish aviators should come to Paris to
45 fetch the machines. . . .

When I went this morning to the Air Ministry everything was going well: when I arrived at the Potez firm the difficulties seemed insurmountable. . . . When Blum went this morning to see the President of the Republic, he found him perturbed and in such a
50 state of mind that he said, 'What is being planned, this delivery of armaments to Spain may mean war or revolution in France', and he asked that an extraordinary Cabinet meeting should be summoned at four o'clock in the afternoon.

The position of the President of the Republic is shared by several
55 Ministers: the Cabinet was divided in its views, and the President of the Chamber, Herriot, has seen Blum and begged him to reflect, for he considered that this has never been done before, and that it may justify a *de facto* recognition by Germany and Italy of any semblance of government set up in a Spanish city and provide it
60 with arms and ammunition in greater quantities than those France can supply. From half-past two till a quarter to four I have been with the Prime Minister and another Minister at the house of a third party: 'My soul is torn,' said Blum, 'I shall maintain my position at all costs and in spite of all risks,' he said. 'We must help
65 Spain that is friendly to us. How? We shall see.'

At 3.30 I again met some of them: the fight had been stern. . . . The resolution of the Cabinet has been to avoid delivery from Government to Government, but to grant us the necessary permits so that private industry may deliver to us. . . .

Spanish envoy in Paris to Giral, the Spanish Prime Minister, quoted in A. Adamthwaite, *The Lost Peace, International Relations in Europe, 1918–1939* (London, Edwin Arnold, 1980), pp 175–7

(d) The American Ambassador on the reasons for the French government's refusal to supply arms to Spain, 27 July 1936

70　Following upon a series of revelations and bitter criticism from the French Right press during the last week, the intricate matter of alleged attempted supply by the Blum government of arms and munitions to the Madrid Government was brought to a focus over the weekend. . . .

75　The reasons which led to the decision were communicated to the Embassy by a reliable press contact who obtained his information from a member of the French Supreme War Council. According to this informant certain members of the Blum Cabinet particularly Cot, Air Minister, decided on July 21 to accede to a request from

80　Spain to send arms and ammunition urgently required by the Madrid Government. . . .

On July 22 Corbin, French Ambassador in London, telephoned Blum personally and called to his attention that the British Government was extremely worried about this contingency.

85　Corbin urged Blum to come over and discuss the situation with Baldwin and Eden as soon as possible. . . . In London Eden drew Blum's attention to the grave international consequences which might result from French active support of the Madrid Government. The fears of the British Government were strengthened by a

90　report from the French Military Intelligence which indicated a certain movement of German troops on the French eastern border. Eden furthermore made it quite clear that he considered that any assistance lent by the French Government to the Spanish Government might conceivably develop a most critical international

95　situation in view of the Italian and German attitude in the matter.

Blum returned to Paris on the 25th and immediately called the Cabinet Council meeting mentioned above in the course of which the British point of view was brought forcibly to the attention of his extremist colleagues, particularly Cot. After a lengthy debate

100　the more moderate elements, Blum, Daladier and Delbos, who advocated a policy of strict neutrality, won out.

> Letter from the American Ambassador in Paris quoted in A. Adamthwaite, *The Making of the Second World War* (London, G. Allen & Unwin, 1977), pp 160–1

(e) Eden denies influencing the French government's decision

(On 28 August) The French Ambassador asked me whether I had any information about the attitude of our own Labour Party on the question of Spain. He rather had the impression that they were not

105　very much interested. I replied that I did not think that this was so, though I had been much intrigued at the story which one of them had brought back from Paris that the suggestion of non-intervention was not originally French but British. I had said that

there was, of course, no truth in this, though I had always thought
110 M. Blum's initiative a wise one. The Ambassador remarked that,
so far as he could recollect, there had been no discussion of the
Spanish problem during our three-power meeting. That is also my
own recollection and the evidence of the records in London.

> A. Eden, *The Eden Memoirs, Facing the Dictators* (London,
> Cassell, 1962), p 406

Questions

a What offices were held in July and August 1936 by Blum,
    Baldwin and Eden?
★ b Why did Hoare consider that the spread of communism to
    Portugal would endanger the British Empire (extract *a*)?
c Which of extracts *a* and *b* do you consider provides the most
    accurate picture of the motives of the British government in
    opting for non-intervention?
★ d Why were the Chiefs of Staff concerned at the prospect of
    Italian control of Spanish Morocco and 'particularly of Ceuta'
    (lines 15–16)?
★ e Explain why, in the context of European diplomacy in the
    summer of 1936, it was considered so important for Britain to
    avoid alienating Italy (lines 26–8)?
f How does extract *d* differ from extract *c* in its account of why
    the French government decided not to aid the Spanish Repub-
    lic? Which explanation do you find most convincing? Is it
    possible to reconcile the two explanations?
g Why would Eden in his *Memoirs* be anxious to deny influencing
    the French government's policy on Spain?
h Assess the usefulness and limitations as evidence to the historian
    of extracts *c, d* and *e*.
★ i Why might the British Labour Party be thought likely to 'take
    an interest' in events in Spain (extract *e*)? What view of the war
    in Spain did they eventually adopt?

4 Soviet aid to the Republic

(a) Stalin's agent in Western Europe describes Soviet motives for assisting the Republic

There was a period of watchful waiting, of furtive exploration.
Stalin wanted to be sure first that there would be no quick and easy
Franco victory. Then he intervened in Spain. His idea was to
include Spain in the sphere of the Kremlin's influence. Such a
5 domination would secure his ties with Paris and London, and thus
strengthen on the other hand his bargaining position with Berlin.
Once he was master of the Spanish Government – of vital strategic

importance to France and Great Britain . . . he would be a force to
be reckoned with, an ally to be coveted. The world believed that
10   Stalin's actions in Spain were in some way connected with world
revolution. But this is not true. The problems of world revolution
had long ago ceased to be real to Stalin. It was solely a question of
Russia's foreign policy. . . . Stalin risked nothing. He took no
chances of involving the Soviet Union in a great war. . . .
15   It was late in August when three high officials of the Spanish
Republic were finally received in Russia. . . . Even now, however,
they were not conveyed to Moscow but kept incognito in a hotel in
Odessa. . . . Stalin called an extraordinary session of the Politbureau
and presented his plan for cautious intervention in the Spanish Civil
20   War. . . . Stalin believed it possible to create in Spain a regime
controlled by him; that done he could command the respect of
France and England, win from them the offer of a real alliance and
either accept it or . . . with that as a bargaining point arrive at his
underlying steady aim and purpose, a compact with Germany.
25   That was Stalin's central thought on Spanish intervention. He was
also moved, however, by the need for some answer to the foreign
friends of the Soviet Union who would be disaffected by the great
purge and the shooting of his old Bolshevik colleagues. . . .
        Two days later a special courier who came by plane to Holland
30   brought the instruction from Moscow. 'Extend your operations
immediately to cover the Spanish Civil War. Mobilise all available
agents and facilities for prompt creation of a system to purchase and
transport arms to Spain.' . . . At the same time Stalin instructed
Yagoda, then Chief of the OGPU, to set up in Spain a branch of the
35   Soviet secret police. . . .
        Stalin's intervention in Spain was now lauched. I went into
action as if I were at the front. . . . Within ten days we had a chain
of brand-new import and export firms established in Paris, London
and other European cities. . . .
40   Captain Oulansky's 'private syndicate' in Odessa . . . called on
Mueller, chief of the OGPU Passport Section, to supply counterfeit
foreign clearance papers. With these false papers, Soviet boats
loaded with munitions would sail from Odessa under new names,
flying foreign colours.

> W. G. Krivitsky, *I was Stalin's Agent* (London, Hamish
> Hamilton, 1939), pp 94–106. (Krivitsky defected to the
> West in late 1937)

(b) The Russian Ambassador's view of Spain, October 1936

45   There is a marked tendency in many quarters to represent the
USSR as intending to try to turn Spain into a Communist
Republic. These suspicions have no basis in fact. Of course the
sympathy of the people of Soviet Russia is on the side of the forces

of the Popular Front now conducting a heroic struggle in Spain and
50   we have no reason to apologise for this. . . .

If the Spanish Government eventually succeeds in suppressing
the rebellion it will not only keep one more country in the camp of
peace, but it will also profoundly influence the whole situation in
Europe by inspiring new confidence in the strength of democracy
55   and in the possibility of the peaceful settlement of international
questions. In this event the danger of war which today looms so
dark on the horizon would be greatly lessened and the political sky
of Europe be cleared of its present clouds.

But if on the contrary, success goes to the rebel generals,
60   supported in contravention of the Non-intervention Agreement by
certain powers, then not only will Spain suffer internal disaster, but
the whole outlook in Europe will be blackened in the last degree,
because the victory of the rebels would mean such a tremendous
encouragement to all the forces of aggression, hatred and destruc-
65   tion in Europe that war would advance to the very threshold of our
homes and engulf our part of the world in the very near future.
This and this alone is the real reason why the Soviet Government
and peoples take the present events in Spain so closely to heart,
their attitude is determined by their policy of peace.

> Statement by Maisky (the Soviet Ambassador to Britain) at
> the Non-Intervention Committee, 30 October 1936; J.
> Degras (ed.), *Soviet Documents of Foreign Policy, vol 3, 1933–
> 41* (London, OUP, 1953), pp 214–15

(c) The Soviet view of non-intervention

70   In adhering with other states to the agreement on non-intervention
in Spanish affairs, the Government of the Soviet Union expected
that it would be observed by its participants, that as a result of this
the period of civil war in Spain would be shortened and the number
of victims reduced.
75   The time that has elapsed since then however, has shown that the
agreement is being systematically violated by a number of
participants, that the supply of arms to the rebels goes unpunished.
One of the parties to the agreement, Portugal, has become the main
supply base for the rebels whilst the legitimate government of
80   Spain has turned out to be, in fact, boycotted, deprived of facilities
to purchase arms outside Spain for the defence of the Spanish
people.
The violation of the agreement has thus created a privileged
situation for the rebels which was certainly not the purpose of the
85   agreement. Thus the agreement has turned out to be an empty,
torn scrap of paper. It has ceased to exist. . . . The Soviet
Government is compelled now to declare that . . . it cannot

consider itself bound by the agreement for non-intervention to any greater extent than any of the other participants of the agreement.

> Degras, *Soviet Documents*, pp 212–13. Maisky, the Soviet Ambassador in London, writing to the Chairman of the Non-Intervention Committee, 24 October 1936

Questions

a   How far is the explanation of Stalin's motives for intervention in Spain in extract *a* supported by the account in extract *b*? To what extent do these extracts support the view that Stalin's foreign policy was motivated by belief in 'socialism in one country'?

b   What indications are there in extract *a* that Krivitsky does not have a high opinion of Stalin?

c   What were the Politbureau (line 18); the OGPU (line 34); and the 'great purge' (lines 27–8)

★ d   How accurate do you consider to be Krivinsky's statement that Stalin in 1936 had the 'underlying aim' of 'a compact with Germany' (line 24)? When and in what circumstances was such a compact made between Germany and the Soviet Union?

★ e   Why was secrecy considered necessary regarding Soviet aid to the Republic?

★ f   What 'danger of war' (line 56) might have been considered to threaten Europe in the autumn of 1936? Was the Soviet assessment of this danger exaggerated?

g   Who were the 'participants' referred to in line 89?

★ h   Why did Portugal aid the Nationalists? By reference to the map on p 36 explain the value to the Nationalists of having Portugal 'as a supply base' (lines 78–9)?

i   How convincingly did Maisky argue in extract *c* that the Non-Intervention Agreement operated to the disadvantage of the Republican government and to the advantage of the Nationalists?

5 The American Secretary of State explains US policy.

On August 7 1936 we telegraphed the Embassy and Consulates in Spain about US Government policy: 'it is clear that our Neutrality Law with respect to embargo of arms, ammunition and implements of war has no application in the present situation, since that
5   applies only in the event of war between or among nations. On the other hand in conforming with its well-established policy of non-intervention in the internal affairs of other countries either in time

of peace or in the event of civil strife, this Government will of
course scrupulously refrain from any interference whatsoever in the
10 unfortunate Spanish situation.' . . . Thus we were applying a
moral embargo. . . .

The President and I were in complete agreement on our policy of
non-intervention in Spain. We believed that the following factors
had to be taken into consideration.
15 The first was that Britain and France had taken the lead in
welding all Europe together into a non-intervention committee.
. . . These nations had only a few hundred miles between them and
Spain. We are 3000 miles away. . . . Europe had rightly taken the
initiative. While twenty-seven nations of Europe had solemnly
20 agreed not to intervene in Spain . . . it would have been unthinkable
for the US to take a contrary course. . . .

The second consideration was that the nations of Europe formed
the Non-Intervention Committee in order to prevent the spread of
the Spanish conflict to the whole continent. We were in sympathy
25 with that aim. . . .

Our third consideration was our own peace and security.
. . . Merely authorising the export of arms to Spain would not be
enough. . . . We should have had to see to it that the arms got to
Spain. . . . This would have meant sending a cruiser along with
30 our shipments. . . . We might well have plunged into the Spanish
war before we realised it. . . .

Memoirs of Cordell Hull (US Secretary of State), (London,
Hodder & Stoughton, 1948), vol 1, pp 478–84

Questions

a   Identify the 'President' (line 12); what do you understand by the
'Neutrality Law' (lines 2–3)?
b   How complete an explanation is given in the extract for the US
government's decision not to intervene in the Civil War?
★   c   To what extent did the Spanish Civil War divide American
public opinion?

6 The International Brigades

(a) Motives for enlisting in the Brigades

During my Summer holiday I had considered going to Spain. My
main objective was fear that I should be no use, that if any
volunteers were needed they would be those who had military
experience. At Wellington College I had been a pacifist and had
5 refused to join the OTC [Officer Training Corps], so I lacked even
that experience. . . .

My job ended on a Friday. On Wednesday I had a party at my flat and auctioned most of the furniture. Altogether I had £9 by the time I left. . . . On Saturday morning a registered letter came by post. I opened it eagerly. It was a formal notice to quit from my landlord's solicitor. I caught the boat-train for Dieppe that night. Ten days later I was in Marseilles; in three weeks at the front.

I do not think anybody does anything just for one clear-cut logical (in this case political), motive. However strongly I sympathised with the cause of the Spanish people, no doubt if my circumstances in London had been completely satisfactory, I should have gone no further than sympathy.

E. Romilly, *Boadilla* (London, Hamish Hamilton, 1937), pp 26–33

(b) Journeying to Spain

The party recruiting office was crowded. Giles [Romilly] and I were soon accepted, but others were an obvious puzzle. Plenty of enthusiasm but hardly one who could fire a weapon. All were taken on. They would be taught. . . .

At Victoria Station the next morning, there was a small crowd to see us off. Mrs Romilly, Communist Party friends, Oxford friends, my family . . . then the whistle went. The train moved. We hung out of the windows, fists clenched. 'Viva Espana!' All clenched fists now, including Nellie Romilly, furcoated. Some heads were high, some were down. Press cameras flashed.

Paris now, and a 'certain address' for another ticket to Perpignan, with food, smokes and cash for the journey. . . . We ate our food, drank a lot of wine and slept. Suddenly, there was Perpignan. We were met by French communists who checked our names and loaded us into trucks. Altogether we made a total of about forty men. A proper meal at a field kitchen, then darkness. A coach arrived; we stumbled in. The coach began to climb very slowly. No smoking. No talking. High up in the Pyrenees came the French frontier. We sat very still. The driver produced a list of names, all Spanish, I learned. Over the Spanish frontier. We could smoke and talk. On to Figueras, where we slept for the night in what might have been a church . . . then came Barcelona, then a train to Albacete, International Brigade headquarters. Finally trucks to Madrigueras, the village a few miles out which was to be our training ground before going into action. A tall young man approached us and checked our names. He then sorted out Giles and myself and said, 'I've been here for two weeks. . . . Welcome to the biggest shambles in Europe.'

T.A.R. Hyndman in P. Toynbee (ed.), *The Distant Drum, Reflections on the Spanish Civil War* (London, Sidgwick & Jackson, 1976) pp 123–4

(c) The members of the Brigades

Another officer was a German . . . from the Thaelmann Battalion. . . . 'I was a Social Democrat in Germany,' he said, 'they put
me in Dachau for a year.' Man after man followed, a little cheerful
Polish Jew had been a clerk in the post office in Warsaw . . . a
50   working man from the Ruhr who had been Communist for years.
He escaped arrest when Hitler came to power. . . . The first man
in International Column uniform whom I heard talking English
might have been the beau ideal of any great public school. . . . He
was a Cambridge graduate. . . . There was John Cornford, a
55   brilliant graduate. These men form one type of British volunteer, –
intellectuals if you like – and the other? There was a Scot who until
a few weeks ago had been a telephonist at a Glasgow hotel.
. . . Another man, a miner, had no experience except marching in
the Hunger March to London . . . [there were] two hard-bitten
60   former members of the IRA who had tasted repression in the days
of the Black and Tans.

> G. Cox, *Defence of Madrid* (London, Gollancz, 1937), pp 85–
> 6, 145–6

Questions

★   *a* Why would German social democrats, Polish jews, Cambridge
graduates and miners enlist in the International Brigades?

★   *b* Explain the reference to the 'Hunger March' (line 59) and
'repression in the days of the Black and Tans' (line 61).

    c What indications are there in extract *b* that the French
government at that time did not actively try to prevent the
movement of volunteers to Spain?

    d Comment on the ways in which the author of extract *b* uses
language to convey a sense of excitment to his readers.

★   *e* What were the total numbers in the International Brigades and
from which nationalities were they mainly recruited?

7 Intellectuals and the war

(a) Stephen Spender gives a writer's view

We were obsessed by the feeling that this was the supreme cause of
our time. The cause of poets and of writers. The cause of freedom.
And that unless the cause of anti-Fascism was won, unless Fascism
was defeated, we would be unable to exist as writers.

> Stephen Spender speaking on an ITV series, *The Spanish
> Civil War*, programme 3, 'Battleground for Idealists', 1982.

(b) War poetry

5   What's your proposal? to build the just city? I will. I agree.
Or is it the suicide pact, the romantic Death? Very well, I accept, for
I am your choice, your decision. Yes I am Spain?

Many have heard it on remote peninsulas,
On sleepy plains, in the aberrant fisherman's islands
10 Or the corrupt heart of the city,
Have heard and migrated like gulls or the seeds of a flower.

They clung like burrs to the long expresses that lurch
Through the unjust lands, through the night, through the alpine
    tunnel
15 They floated over the oceans;
They walked the passes. All presented their lives.

To-morrow the rediscovery of romantic love,
The photographing of ravens; all the fun under
Liberty's masterful shadow;
20 To-morrow the hour of the pageant-master and the musician.

The beautiful roar of the chorus under the dome;
To-morrow the exchanging of tips on the breeding of terriers.
The eager election of chairmen
By the sudden forest of hands. But today the struggle.

25 To-morrow for the young the poets exploding like bombs,
The walks by the lake, the weeks of perfect communion;
To-morrow the bicycle races
Through the suburbs on summers evenings. But today the struggle.

> Verses from W. H. Auden, 'Spain' 1937, quoted in V. Cunningham (ed.), *Spanish Front, Writers on the Civil War* (Oxford University Press, Oxford, 1986) pp 3–4

Questions

a In what ways does Auden's poem present a similar view of the Civil War to Spender's statement?
b Comment on the effectiveness of the style of Auden's poem.
c Assess the value of poetry as evidence for the historian.

IV   The War from August 1936 to March 1937

Introduction

The military events of the Spanish Civil War often give an impression of ill-prepared improvisation. Both armies lacked experience, training, modern weapons, tanks and aircraft, though the Nationalists were gradually to acquire superiority in manpower and technology. While the war 'offered a preview of the new tactics and equipment that would be the hallmarks of a major European war' (Browne), the static trench warfare along much of the front line more greatly resembled the battles of the First World War than those of the Second. On the Republican side the revolt led to a complete breakdown in military organisation as the regular army was replaced by the 'revolutionary warfare' of militia units responsible only to the different political parties. Only in October 1936 did Caballero's government begin to establish a new, disciplined Popular Army based on the Communist Fifth Regiment.

The Nationalists with their more conventional organisation, Moors and Foreign Legion, fared better but at first they also lacked men and ammunition.

According to G. Hills (*Battle for Madrid*), the Republicans made numerous military blunders; 'obsessed with the defence of Madrid', they adopted a passive strategy instead of immediately advancing southwards to prevent Franco from establishing a bridgehead in Algeciras and consolidating his position in Seville.

Franco and Mola were able to join forces by October 1936, driving the inexperienced militias before them. There was much argument, then and later, over whether the war could best be won by militias or by a disciplined army but historians now generally agree that the militias were no match for the professionals of Franco's army: 'On the one hand it is true that the popular enthusiasm associated with Revolutions was a major factor in the initial resistance to the Nationalists. On the other, there is no proof that such enthusiasm could be effectively channelled into a victory over Franco' (Paul Heywood).

Both sides introduced regimes of terror in the areas of Spain they controlled, Nationalist repression including the killing of the poet Lorca in Granada. Each accused the other of atrocities while minimising their own actions. There were differences, however, and recent research concludes that while Nationalist terror lasted throughout the war (and after), terror in the Republican areas was at its height in the early days of the war and then declined with the reassertion of republican legality. 'On the Nationalist side terror was a matter of policy . . . while on the Republican side such tactics were officially deplored and increasingly curbed' (H. Browne).

In November 1936 Franco launched an attack on Madrid, delayed (perhaps crucially) by his decision to relieve the fortress of the Alcazar in Toledo where a small Nationalist force was holding out against the Republicans. The Alcazar became one of the epics of Civil War history but it illustrates the view that 'both sides sacrificed lives and wasted time in unnecessary campaigns to gain militarily unimportant objectives'. The Germans and Italians were to become impatient with what they saw as Franco's dogged and uninspired leadership. Some historians consider that Madrid was strategically unimportant but its symbolic significance to both sides cannot be discounted.

The successful defence of Madrid, entrusted to General Miaja while the government fled to Valencia, has been variously credited by historians to the International Brigades, Soviet aid (which, arriving in October, gave the Republic a temporary advantage), 'the courage and sacrifice of the Madrid People' or to the government having 'more men and material than the Nationalists'.

At the end of November Franco ceased direct attacks on the city in favour of gradual encirclement. In February 1937 the Nationalists attempted to cut the Madrid–Valencia road in the battle of the river Jarama and in March Italian troops were involved in an unsuccessful attack from the north-east at Guadalajara.

The war appeared to have reached a stalemate, though the Nationalists had made more gains than their opponents, capturing Irun on the French frontier in August 1936 and Malaga in February 1937.

However, this impasse was to be broken when Franco in March 1937 took a crucial decision to abandon attacks on Madrid in favour of what has been described as 'the decisive campaign of the war' – the conquest of the industrially vital Asturias and the Basque country in northern Spain.

1 Terror and repression

(a) Nationalist terror in Badajoz, August 1936

This is the most painful story it has ever been my lot to handle. . . .

I have come from Badajoz, several miles away in Spain. I have been up on the roof to look back. There was a fire. They are burning bodies. Four thousand men and women have died at Badajoz since General Francisco Franco's Rebel Foreign Legionnaires and Moors climbed over the bodies of their own dead through its many times blood-drenched walls. . . .

We drove straight to the Plaza. Here yesterday there was a ceremonial, symbolic shooting. Seven leading Republicans of the Popular Front shot with a band and everything before three thousand people. To prove that Rebel generals didn't shoot only workers and peasants. . . .

Suddenly we saw two Phalangists halt a strapping fellow in a workman's blouse and hold him while a third pulled back his shirt, baring his right shoulder. The black and blue marks of a rifle butt could be seen. Even after a week they showed. The report was unfavourable. To the bull ring with him.

We drove out along the walls to the ring in question. . . . It is a fine ring of white plaster and red brick. I saw Juan Belmonte [a bullfight idol], here once on the eve of the fight on a night like this, when he came down to watch the bulls brought in. This night the fodder for tomorrow's show was being brought in too. Files of men, arms in the air.

They were young, mostly peasants in blue blouses, mechanics in jumpers. 'The Reds.' They are still being rounded up. At four o'clock in the morning they are turned out into the ring through the gate by which the initial parade of the bullfight enters. There machine guns await them.

> Jay Allen in the *Chicago Tribune*, 30 August 1936, quoted in Cunningham (ed.), *Spanish Front, Writers on the Civil War*, pp 103–6

(b) A revolutionary tribunal in Madrid, August 1936

While we were chatting, another man entered, in the forties, with a fierce mustache, black and crooked teeth and lively gray eyes. His *Salud* sounded more like the growl of a dog than a salute and he started at once to swear, displaying an inexhaustible vocabulary of blasphemies. When he had vented his bad temper he dropped heavily into a chair and stared at us.

'Well,' he said after a while, 'today we'll liquidate all the Fascists we've got here. A pity it's only half a dozen, I'd prefer six dozen'. . . .

The young Miliciano, 'Little Paws' and a third taciturn man constituted themselves a People's Tribunal, with Antonio as counsel for the defence. Two Milicianos brought in the first prisoner, a twenty-year old boy, his elegant suit dirty with dust and cobwebs and his eyelids reddened.

'Come nearer, my fine bird, we won't eat you,' Little Paws jeered at him.

45   The militiaman in the armchair took a list from the desk and read out the name and details. The accused belonged to the Falange; several comrades had seen him selling Fascist newspapers and on two occasions he had taken part in street fights. When he was arrested, a lead bludgeon, a pistol and a Falange membership card

50   were found on him.

'What have you to say for yourself?' the judge in the chair asked.

'Nothing. I've had bad luck.' The prisoner fell back into a defiant silence, his head bent, his hands rubbing against each other. Little Paws leaned forward from his chair:

55   'All right. Take him away and bring the next one.'

When we were alone the judge asked: 'Are we all agreed?'

The three of them and Antonio answered in the affirmative; the Fascist would be taken out and shot that night.

A. Barea, *Forging of a Rebel* (London, Davis-Poynter, 1972), pp 558–9. (The autobiography of a Spaniard who worked in Madrid during the Civil War as head of the Republican Foreign Press Department)

Questions

a   What evidence is there in these extracts to support the view that both sides in the Civil War were equally ruthless in exterminating their political opponents?

b   Comment on the effectiveness of the style of extract *a*.

★ c   Why do you think that terror and cruelty to the civilian population were such pronounced features of the Spanish Civil War?

★ d   Comment on the accuracy of the term 'Reds' (line 25), to describe the supporters of the Republic and of the term 'fascist' (line 35), to describe supporters of the Nationalists.

2 Military organisation

(a) The problems of Republican army organisation in July 1936

The office [militia supply in Madrid] was an inferno, not only because of the stifling heat and the incessant ringing of six telephones but mainly on account of the people of all sorts who were everlastingly coming and going. . . . First of all they wanted

5   arms and ammunition. After the bona fides of every applicant had been rigorously checked arms were alloted them through the various political parties and organisations. 60,000 rifles were distributed in this way. . . .

The nights were terrible. We generally spent them appealing to

10   the political parties to let us have armed men to relieve the pressure
      on one or other of the fronts from which desperate appeals kept
      pouring in. . . . We also had to provide against the possibility of
      risings by the civil guards. . . .
          On the whole the problem of the feeding of the troops was one
15   of those which were most effectively solved. . . . The greatest
      problem was the lack of means of transport. Though thousands of
      lorries had been requisitioned, lorries were never available when
      we had a convoy ready to go to the front. A road transport
      committee had been formed on a trade union basis for the purpose
20   of organising transport to the front line . . . inevitably the drivers
      did not obey the committee's orders. . . .
          I remember seeing a crowd of officers waiting outside the
      Minister's doors. They had all applied for permission to serve the
      Republic and the tragedy of their situation was painted on their
25   faces. They were only too well aware that if their services were
      rejected their lives would be in danger. An F [for fascist] put beside
      a man's name was often equivalent to a death sentence. . . .
          So great was the shortage of material that the distribution of the
      available supply was controlled from the Minister's own office.
30   . . . Not a single day passed without the War Minister being
      haunted by the shortage of munitions. . . .
          There was of course no general staff but its functions were partly
      fulfilled by the Intelligence Department which received all cable
      and wireless messages. . . . Most of the other departments of the
35   general staff were not created until after 5 September when
      Caballero became Minister of War. We had a lot of trouble in
      securing a 155 mm gun for Toledo. . . . However we obtained it in
      the end and we were at last in a position to carry out a
      bombardment of the famous Alcazar of Toledo. But there was not
40   a single officer who knew how to use the gun. . . .
              J. M. Blazquez, *I Helped Build an Army* (London, Secker &
              Warburg, 1939), pp 125–50

(b) Two views of the militias on the Aragon front

(i) A republican officer's experience of the militias in August 1936

On approaching Sarinena I came across a truck halted on the other
side of the highway, and at the request of a group of soldiers
stopped my car. Their truck had broken down, but they did not
know what was wrong with it. . . .
45   'Where are you going?' I asked them with surprise.
      'To Barcelona to spend the Sunday there.'
      'But aren't you supposed to be at the front?'
      'Sure, but as there's nothing doing we are going to Barcelona.'
      'Have you been given leave?'

50   'No. Can't you see we are militiamen?'
  •   The commander of the Aragon front recommended that a decisive operation be launched against Huesca. Everything pointed to the fact that this historic Aragonese town was almost without protection and that with an intelligent and well-coordinated attack
55   it would have fallen into the hands of the Republic. Those present listened to his plan, which was discussed in detail, but unfortunately they finally decided to consult their respective trade-union organisations before accepting anything. In the end the discussion took a very regrettable turn because the commander's request that
60   some of the columns should hand over to other units the additional material they needed was rejected out of hand.

    Quoted in Bolloten, *The Spanish Revolution,* pp 246–7

(ii) In support of the militias

  • • Most of the army was with the fascists. It must be confronted by a new army. Every workers' organisation proceeded to organise militia regiments, equip them and send them to the front. The
65   government had no direct contact with the workers' militia
. . . such officers as remained in the Loyalist camp were assigned as 'technicians' to the militias. . . .

    Much malicious propaganda has been spread by the Stalinists concerning the alleged weakness of the military activity of the
70   anarchists. The hasty creation of militias, the organisation of the war industry, were inevitably haphazard in all unaccustomed hands. But in those first months, the anarchists, seconded by the POUM, made up for much of their military inexperience by their bold social policies. In civil war, politics is the determining
75   weapon. By taking the initiative, by seizing the factories, by organising the peasantry to take the land, the CNT masses crushed the Catalonian garrisons, By marching into Aragon as social liberators, they roused the peasantry to paralyse the mobility of the fascist forces. In the plans of the generals, Saragossa . . . was to
80   have been for Eastern Spain what Burgos became in the west. Instead Saragossa was immobilised from the first days . . . the POUM reprinted for distribution in the militias the original Red Army Manual of Trotsky, providing for a democratic internal regime and political life in the army.

    F. Morrow (an American supporter of the POUM), *Revolution and Counter-revolution in Spain* (London, New Park Publications, 1963), pp 19–22, 70

(c) The arming of the International Brigades

85   After several weeks of being weaponless we started to receive a most extraordinary variety of automatic weapons. The first of these was always known as a 'shosser'. . . . There seemed to be an

almost unlimited number of ways it could jam itself which it
usually succeeded in doing before it had fired more than five
90   consecutive rounds. . . . They were not one of the Government's
best buys. The best of the automatic weapons which we received
were eight Maxims. They were very old, none bearing a date later
than 1916, but they were ruggedly constructed. . . . When the
Battalion finally went into action for the first time it was heavily
95   armed with largely useless automatic weapons apart from the
Maxims. The remaining infantry was supplied with rifles of
Russian manufacture. These were very poor weapons, much
lighter than the English Lee-Enfield of that period and not nearly as
toughly constructed . . . we were instructed that the rifle should
100 only be fired with the bayonet in position. This was hopelessly
impractical and all the bayonets were lost or discarded within a
couple of days up at the Front. . . .

J. Gurney, *Crusade in Spain* (London, Faber, 1974), pp 61–79

(d) An English volunteer describes the Nationalist army in November 1936

We were admitted as Requetes [to the cavalry], without, so far as I
remember, the formality of signing a single document. . . . We
105 drew no pay and we had to buy our own uniforms for the stores
had none left. . . . The men it seemed were from Andalusia, all of
them volunteers. . . . Captain Llancia Manques de Cocuhuella said
they were the simplest type of peasant, usually obedient and
cheerful but easily depressed, inefficient and inclined to be lazy – on
110 the whole little different from children. I was given a horse
. . . also an old Mauser carbine and a sabre. . . . The only
automatic weapon the squadron possessed was one old Hotchkiss
light machine gun; I belive that there were two people in the
Squadron who knew how to use it.
115   Llancia explained to me that the Squadron was well below
strength. . . . The Squadron operational duties were the protection
of a sector of the Talavera-Toledo road . . . the road was very
thinly held. . . .
        I learnt one thing about the Requetes; for all their courage and
120 endurance, their patriotism and self-sacrificing idealism, they
lacked the strict discipline and technical training which are so
necessary in modern warfare. Only in the foreign legion, I was
convinced, could I hope to learn first class soldiering. . . . They
were the troops on whom General Franco depended for the most
125 difficult operations. . . . This was the corps d'élite of the Spanish
army. Major de Mora was a superb commander and a brilliant
tactician. . . . The chaplain was a regular army padre . . . he was
greatly relieved when I assured him that I was not a Freemason. . . .
        As in all banderas [of the foreign legion] the men were 90%

130   Spanish. The remainder were mostly Portuguese . . . the legionar-
ies like their officers were all volunteers . . . discipline on duty and
in the field was extremely strict, even savage by English standards.
        P. Kemp, *Mine Were of Trouble* (London, Cassell, 1957), pp
        40–5, 103–18

Questions

 a   What is meant by 'the Stalinists' (line 68)?
 b   Why was the foreign legion described as the 'corps d'élite' (line
       125) of the Spanish army?
 c   What is meant by the 'original Red Army Manual of Trotsky'
       (lines 82–3) and why did the POUM regard it as sufficiently
       important to be distributed to the troops?
 d   What evidence is there in extracts *a* and *b* to illustrate
       Republican suspicion of regular army officers?
 e   What did the writer of extract *b* (ii) mean by the statement 'in
       civil war, *politics* is the determining weapon' (lines 74–5), and
       how is this idea illustrated in the extract?
 f   How effectively does extract *b* (ii) answer the complaints about
       the militias made in *b* (i)?
 g   What, according to extracts *a, b* and *c* were the main military
       problems facing the Republic in the autumn of 1936?
 h   What do the extracts disclose of the differences between the
       Nationalist and Republican armies?
 i   How far do these extracts support the view that the Nationalist
       armies were superior in equipment and organisation to those of
       the Republic?
 j   Why were the Republicans attacking the 'Alcazar of Toledo'
       (line 39) and what was the outcome of this battle?
★   k   What strategy did Franco and Mola adopt in the first few weeks
       of the war and how successful were they?

3 The Aragon Front

The front line here was not a continuous line of trenches, which
would have been impossible in such mountainous country; it was
simply a chain of fortified posts, always known as 'positions'
perched on each hill-top. . . . The position was a semi-circular
5   enclosure about fifty yards across, with a parapet that was partly
sandbags and partly lumps of limestone. There were thirty or forty
dug-outs running into the ground like ratholes . . . there were
twelve sentries placed in various points in the trench and behind the
inner parapet. In front of the trench was the barbed wire and then
10   the hillside slid down into a seemingly bottomless ravine; opposite
were naked hills, in places mere cliffs of rock, all grey and wintry,

with no life anywhere, not even a bird. I peered cautiously through
a loophole, trying to find the Fascist trench.

'Where are the enemy?'

15   Benjamin waved his hand expansively. 'Over there.'

'But *where*?'

According to my ideas of trench warfare the Fascists would be
fifty or a hundred yards away. I could see nothing – seemingly their
trenches were very well concealed. Then with a shock of dismay I
20   saw where Benjamin was pointing; on the opposite hill-top beyond
the ravine, 700 metres away at the very least, the tiny outline of a
parapet and a red-and-yellow flag – the Fascist position. I was
indescribably disappointed. We were nowhere near them! At that
range our rifles were completely useless. . . .

25   Up here in the hills round Saragossa, it was simply the mingled
boredom and discomfort of stationary warfare. . . . On every hill-
top, Fascist or Loyalist, a knot of ragged, dirty men, shivering
round their flag and trying to keep warm. And all day and night
meaningless bullets wandering across the empty valleys and only
30   by some rare, improbable chance getting home on a human body.
. . . The front line, ours and the Fascists, lay in positions of
immense natural strength, which as a rule could only be
approached from one side. Provided a few trenches have been dug,
such places cannot be taken by infantry except in overwhelming
35   numbers. . . . We would have made lovely marks for artillery but
there was no artillery. . . . The Fascists did occasionally manage to
bring a gun or two from Saragossa and fire a few shells, so few that
they never even found the range and the shells plunged harmlessly
into the empty ravines.

G. Orwell, *Homage to Catalonia* (London, Martin Secker &
Warburg, 1970) pp 29–40

Questions

a   What does this extract reveal of the lack of military resources of
both sides in the Civil War?

b   What evidence is there in this extract to support the view that
the military situation in the Spanish Civil War resembled that of
the First World War?

4 The battle for Madrid

(a) Republican proclamation 6 November 1936

• Madrid will be the tomb of fascism.

No pasaran!

Every house a fortress, every street a trench, every neighbourhood a wall of iron and combatants. . . .

5 Emulate Petrograd! 7 November on the Manzanares must be as glorious as on the Neva!

Wives – tomorrow prepare to take your husbands' lunch to the trenches, not to the factory.

Viva Madrid without a government.

> Quoted in Fraser, *Blood of Spain*, p 255

(b) The Commander of the British Battalion describes the defence of Madrid

10 Franco launched his forces in a frontal attack on the city about 7 November through the park, the Casa del Campo, that covers all the 'West End' of Madrid. . . . As his troops entered on one side of the Casa del Campo the first of our International Brigades marched across one of Madrid's bridges to entrench themselves in the park.
15 They had been very hastily organised. They had very few machine-guns . . . they had a job lot of rifles. But they knew a good deal about fighting. . . .

Don't let us exaggerate; our Brigades did not save Madrid. Madrid would have saved itself without us. But without us Franco
20 would have got farther into Madrid; he would have crossed the Casa del Campo and forced his way into the streets of the city itself. There street-fighting would have stopped him. . . .

Franco's troops got across the little river that flows between Casa del Campo and Madrid. They got into a group of big buildings
25 isolated from the city by some open ground, called the University City. . . . An extraordinary sort of fighting developed in these tall buildings six or eight storeys high. Sometimes we would be holding the top floors and sniping from the roofs while Moors were holding the lower floors; sometimes it was the other way
30 round.

> Tom Wintringham, *English Captain* (London, Faber & Faber, 1939), pp 134–7

(c) A reporter describes the battle for Madrid

From the Fifth Regiment come orders telling householders to fill bottles with petrol and cork them with cotton wool. This is to be lighted and flung at tanks and armoured cars from roof-tops and windows. House committees are organised for every dwelling to
35 comb out fifth columnists. Shooting at shadows is forbidden in the streets. People are organised for barricade construction. . . .

Franco's first attack on Madrid had failed. . . . One great reason for this check was that the rebels had not enough men. His advance from the south-west had been accomplished with a force of not
40 more than 25,000 men . . . it depended for its striking force on

outside aid. . . . He had a definite superiority in armaments, particularly in tanks, machine-guns, bombers, anti-aircraft guns . . . but it was clear that he could capture Madrid only if the defence crumpled up suddenly or he could find an open enough
45   route to the centre of the city so that his tanks and armoured cars could protect his small forces. For against him the Government had some 35,000 men in the militias and at least 75,000 armed men in Madrid who could be called on in a house-to-house struggle. . . . It was clear that Franco's 30,000 however efficient . . . would be
50   annihilated if they penetrated into streets where every window had its rifle.

    Why did Franco not bring up more men? His long line of communications from Toledo to Talavera was still sufficiently threatened by Government troops to force him to keep locked up
55   thousands of troops in villages and towns along the route as garrisons against counter-attack. He had to face the threat of increased pressure from Basques in the north on Oviedo and on the Aragon front. And thousands of men had to be kept behind the lines to control the territory he had conquered. The people fought
60   and had shown that they were prepared to fight further. Their position was much stronger in the city confines than it had been in the open field. They were fighting now on short internal lines of communication . . . troops and supplies could be shifted by tram if need be. Men could be fed in restaurants and cafes instead of
65   makeshift field kitchens . . . headquarters were near and co-ordination easier. . . . The Junta was free too, to some degree, from the inter-party jealousies and struggle for power of the Cabinet.

        Cox, *Defence of Madrid*, pp 82–110

(d) Germany recognises Franco's government

  • Since the Government of General Franco has taken possession of
70   the greater part of the Spanish national territory and since developments of the past weeks have shown more and more clearly that no responsible government authority can be said to exist any longer in the rest of Spain, the German Government has decided to recognise the Government of General Franco and to appoint a
75   chargé d'affaires to it for the purpose of taking up diplomatic relations.

        Documents on German Foreign Policy, Series D, Volume 1, text of communqué 18 November 1936, p 132

Questions

  • *a* What is meant by 'no pasaran' (line 2)?
  ★ *b* Explain the reference to 'emulate Petrograd! 7 November on the Manzanares must be as glorious as on the Neva!' (lines 5–6).

c   What is meant by 'Madrid without a government' (line 9); 'fifth regiment' (line 31)?
d   Explain the reference to 'fifth columnists' (line 35).
e   Different historians have concluded that 'victory was that of the populace of Madrid' (Thomas), and that 'the 11th International Brigade was vital to the defence of Madrid' (Preston). Comment on these views in the light of the evidence in the extracts.
f   What do the authors of extracts b and c suggest are the most important reasons for the Nationalist failure to capture Madrid? On what points do these extracts support one another?
★ g   How accurate was the view of the situation in Spain in November 1936 given by the German Government in extract d?

5 The Battle of Jarama, February 1937

(a) An account of the battle on 12 February by a member of the International Brigade

About two miles ahead was the Jarama river . . . it was obvious that Franco's forces had already crossed the river in considerable strength. . . . It was obvious that this was going to be a bloody and hard-fought affair but the propaganda machine had so reduced the
5   reality of the situation that we were convinced that we had only to advance for the enemy immediately to retreat. Nobody at Madrigueras had said anything about artillery fire or the genius of Moorish infantry to move across country without presenting a target for anyone but a highly trained marksman. . . .
10   [At the Brigade HQ] Gal gave what was clearly a momentous order . . . that the Battalion should advance immediately along the whole line of our frontage. I explained that we had still made no contact with the Franco-Belge Battalion who were supposed to be occupying a position on our right flank, and was told that they
15   were already in position and had commenced their advance. I knew damned well that this was nonsense as I had come down via their supposed position, but who was I to argue with a Russian Brigadier?
    I got back to Wintringham's HQ and relayed the Brigadier's
20   orders. Runners were sent out to 1, 3 and 4 Companies to order the advance . . . William Briskey's No 3 Company on the Casa Blanca hill was the first to move down the hill from its summit, followed shortly after by No 1 Company under Kit Conway. But I could see no sign of Overton and No 4 Company as they were concealed
25   from me by a fold in the ground. Suddenly and without any warning, all hell broke loose under a storm of artillery and heavy machine-gun fire. It concentrated first on the Casa Blanca hill which became completely obscured in clouds of smoke and dust.

The barrage was continued for about three hours. . . . I could see
30 the chaos of Casa Blanca hill where some of the men were working
away with bayonet and tin helmet in an attempt to produce some
sort of fox-hole in which to hide. . . .
During a lull in the firing Wintringham sent me down to the
Casa Blanca hill to get a situation report from Briskey as we had
35 received no word from him since the barrage started. I went along
the sunken road and made my wat across the dead ground in the
rear of the hill. . . . When I reached the crest of the hill, the scene I
found was really horrible. Briskey was dead and No 3 Company
had lost more than half its total strength. . . . The situation in
40 Overton's Company was worse. . . .
I found Wintringham up in No 2 Company's trench and told him
what I could of the situation. As we sat there we were able to watch
the Moorish advance. What was left of our three companies were
showing tremendous spirit but there was no machine gun fire and
45 only the occasional bark of a shosser letting off a few rounds before
it jammed again. There must have been at least three battalions of
Moors and their movement was amazingly skilful. . . . The effect
of those brown, ferocious bundles suddenly appearing out of the
ground at one's feet was utterly demoralising. . . . They were
50 professionals, backed by a mass of artillery and heavy machine-gun
fire supplied by the German Condor legion. It was a formidable
opposition to be faced by a collection of city-bred young men with
no experience of war, no idea how to find cover on an open hillside
and no competence as marksmen. . . .
55 Wintringham had tried to persuade Gal to agree to withdraw to
the line of the sunken road – but the line must be held 'at all costs',
any retreat would be met with court martial and all manner of dire
penalties. . . .
     Gurney, *Crusade in Spain*, pp 101–9

(b) An account of the battle on 17 and 18 February by a Nationalist volunteer

At dawn on the morning of 17 February we awoke to the sound of
60 heavy firing away to our left. We ran to our trenches and took up
firing positions. . . . As the haze rolled back in the rising sun we
saw groups of little dark figures moving towards us. . . . We held
our fire letting them reach the olive trees undisturbed. Surely, I
thought, they can't mean to attack across those open fields in front
65 with no artillery preparation? It's sheer suicide although they do
outnumber us many times. But in a moment they emerged from
cover and began to advance at a trot towards us. We waited until
they were well in the open, then our machine guns opened up; we
joined in with our rifles. The little trotting figures halted and
70 toppled down in heaps . . . soon they were running back to shelter

leaving their dead and wounded strewn among the stubble. . . .

Suddenly we heard the sound of heavy tanks and from our right approached six Russian tanks each carrying a thirty-seven milli-metre gun in its turret. This looked awkward for us, and would
75 have been if any infantry had followed them; but the latter had no fight left in them. If the tanks had preceded the earlier attack the result might have been very different. . . .

At that moment our artillery came into action. It found the range all round the tanks. They wavered, then came to a halt. A moment
80 later one of them was enveloped in black smoke as a shell struck it squarely; it began to burn. Then another was hit at the base of the turret. The remaining four, turned, spread out and made off.

Next day there was another Republican attack. . . . I saw Frejo and Santo Domingo on top of the parapets, each standing behind
85 his men, each wearing his red beret and wrapped in a capote, unmoved by the bullets flying around him . . . this was the true Requete tradition. It was nearly noon. There seemed no prospect of reinforcements for us, our ammunition was running low and the enemy now within 300 yards of us was preparing for the final
90 assault. . . . Then we heard a new sound of tank engines. In a few moments a column of our own light tanks (German tanks though the crew were Spanish) . . . came into view, about sixteen of them, each with two machine-guns . . . the battle was decided. The Republicans had no chance caught between our fire and the
95 guns of the tanks, they were shot down in swathes. . . .

Kemp, *Mine Were of Trouble*, pp 73–80

Questions

a   Explain what is meant in extract *a* by: 'propaganda machine' (line 4).
b   According to extracts *a* and *b* what advantages did the Nationalists possess in the Battle of Jarama and what mistakes did the Republicans make?
c   What evidence is there in extract *a* to indicate that the writer had become disillusioned with the war in Spain?
d   What do the extracts reveal of the importance of foreign aid to both sides in this battle?
e   Explain what is meant by 'the true Requete tradition' (lines 86–7)?

6 A British newspaper account of the Battle of Guadalajara, March 1937

Italy's Second 'Caporetto'
Retreat goes on
Italians 'useless in Spain'
Spanish Government troops continue to advance north-east of

5   Madrid and the collapse of the Italian army is now fully confirmed. Vast quantities of equipment and munitions were thrown away or left behind.

It is thought that the Italians have not suffered heavy losses as they appear in the main to have kept out of the reach of the
10 Government troops.

A special correspondent of the Press Association who has visited the front described it as a 'second Caporetto'. The correspondent says that the country is ideal for mechanised units, but the cold has destroyed the morale of the rebels. He says that the Italians are
15 useless in such a climate.

        Manchester Guardian, 22 March 1937

Questions

★   *a* Explain the reference to a 'second Caporetto' (lines 1 and 12).
    b What does the writer of this report reveal of his attitude towards the Italians in Spain?
★   *c* Why was the Nationalist offensive at Guadalajara unsuccessful?

7 Franco's tactics in April 1937

(a) Franco's conversation with the Italian Ambassador, 18 April 1937

I must not exterminate the enemy or destroy cities, the country-side, industries and production. For that reason I must not be in a hurry. If I were in a hurry, I should be a bad Spaniard. If I were in a hurry, I should not be a patriot but would be behaving like a
5 foreigner. . . .

The thwarted offensives on Madrid have taught me that I have to abandon my programme of total, grandiose and immediate liberation. Region after region, success after success; the people on the other side will understand and will know how to wait. No
10 amount of argument will make me depart from this gradual programme. There will be less glory but more internal peace afterwards. After each of my successes there will be fewer Reds in front of me and behind me as well. Seen in this light the civil war could last another year, two or perhaps three. . . .

15   Give me planes, give me artillery, give me tanks and ammunition, give me your diplomatic support, and I shall be very grateful. But above all do not make me hurry, do not oblige me to win at top speed, for this would mean killing more Spaniards, destroying a greater part of the national wealth, and in consequence, to make
20 the foundations of my government ever more unsteady.

        Crozier, *Franco*, pp 244–5

(b) Mussolini's view of the Nationalists

In a conversation Mussolini expressed himself as greatly dissatisfied with the achievements of the Spanish Nationalists. They were obviously lacking in offensive spirit and also in personal bravery. There were evidently very few real men in Spain.

> *Documents on German Foreign Policy*, letter from the German Ambassador in Rome to the Foreign Office, 25 November 1936, p 139

Questions

a   What arguments did Franco put forward in extract *a* to justify his cautious strategy?

b   Explain why Franco refered to 'foreigners' (line 5).

c   Explain the reference to 'the people on the other side' (line 9).

d   What impression do these extracts convey of Nationalist relations with the Italians?

e   Comment on Mussolini's view of the war in the light of the account of the battle of Guadalajara given in the previous extract.

f   What does extract *b* reveal of Mussolini's character?

g   Comment on the accuracy of Franco's statement that the 'war could last another year, two or perhaps three'.

★ h   What military gains had the Nationalists made between July 1936 and March 1937?

★ i   What new military campaign had Franco already embarked on by April 1937 and why had he done so?

V Republican Spain

Introduction

In Republican Spain the rising precipitated precisely that revolution which the rebels had hoped to prevent. The atmosphere of revolutionary euphoria in Barcelona was graphically described by George Orwell. In Catalonia and Aragon the authority of the central government collapsed and the various working-class parties and their militias took control. In the summer and autumn of 1936 much of the industry and agriculture in these areas was collectivised, many of the former owners having fled.

In September 1936 Caballero, the UGT leader, became Prime Minister of a left-wing government which included Socialists, Communists and eventually, against their political inclinations, the Anarchists.

But political unity in the Republic was difficult to achieve. The main dispute centred on whether 'victory over Franco was a necessary precursor to revolution or whether Revolution was the only means by which to achieve that victory'.

The former view eventually prevailed. Because of the importance of Soviet aid and because they advocated efficient pursuit of the war, the Communist Party quickly gained ground, increasing its membership from 10,000 in February 1936 to over 1,000,000 by July 1937. The Communists and Socialists in Catalonia had already merged their parties. The Communists, however, had no desire to establish a Soviet regime in Spain and sought successfully to curb the revolution, fearing to alienate Britain and France whose support Stalin needed against Germany.

Political tension came to a head in May 1937 in four days of fighting in Barcelona between the POUM (a Marxist, anti-Stalinist group regarded as Trotskyist by the Communists) and the CNT on the one hand, and the Communists and their Socialist allies on the other. This 'civil war within the civil war' which began ostensibly as a conflict over control of the Barcelona telephone exchange, resulted in the defeat of the POUM and their eventual suppression by the Communist secret police. Shortly afterwards Caballero, who had come to resent Communist influence, was replaced as Prime Minister by Negrin, a former Physiology Professor who had been Minister for Finance. Negrin has been variously described as either a Communist dupe or as an astute politician 'performing a delicate and dangerous balancing act' (Carr) in order to preserve his independence while continuing to receive Soviet aid.

Certainly political disunity and its effect on military decisions can be regarded as a major reason for the defeat of the Republic. The role of the Communists and the Soviet Union is still hotly debated. Did Communist efficiency stave off defeat, in the words of Paul Preston, 'playing a major role in keeping Republican resistance alive as long as it did', or did Soviet domination accompanied by purges of opponents demoralise Republicans and pave the way for Franco's success?

1 The Revolution

(a) Revolutionary Barcelona

This was in late December 1936 . . . the Anarchists were still in virtual control of Catalonia and the revolution was still in full-swing. It was the first time that I had ever been in a town where the working class was in the saddle. Practically every building of any
5   size had been seized by the workers and was draped with red flags or with the red and black flag of the Anarchists; every wall was scrawled with the hammer and sickle and with the initials of the revolutionary parties; almost every church had been gutted and its images burnt. Churches here and there were being systematically
10 demolished by gangs of workmen.

Every shop and cafe had an inscription saying that it had been collectivised; even the bootblacks had been collectivised and their boxes painted red and black. Waiters and shop-walkers looked you in the face and treated you as an equal. . . . Nobody said 'Senor' or
15 'Don'; everyone called everyone else 'Comrade' and 'Thou' and said 'Salud!' instead of 'Buenos dias'. Tipping was forbidden by law. . . . There were no private motor-cars, they had all been commandeered, and all the trams and taxis and much of the other transport were painted red and black.
20 The revolutionary posters were everywhere, flaming from the walls in clean reds and blues that made the few remaining advertisements look like daubs of mud. Down the Ramblas, the wide central artery of the town where crowds of people streamed constantly to and fro, the loudspeakers were bellowing revolutionary
25 songs all day and far into the night. . . . In outward appearance it was a town in which the wealthy classes had practically ceased to exist . . . practically everyone wore rough working-class clothes or blue overalls, or some variant of the militia uniform.

All this was queer and moving. There was much in it that I did

30 not understand, in some ways did not even like, but I recognised it
immediately as a state of affairs worth fighting for. Also I believed
that things were as they appeared, that this was really a workers'
state and that the entire bourgeoisie had either fled, been killed, or
voluntarily come over to the workers' side; I did not realise that
35 great numbers of well-to-do bourgeois were simply lying low and
disguising themselves as proletarians for the time being. . . . There
was a belief in the revolution and the future, a feeling of having
suddenly emerged into an era of equality and freedom. Human
beings were trying to behave as human beings and not as cogs in
40 the capitalist machine. In the barbers' shops there were Anarchist
notices solemnly explaining that barbers were no longer slaves.
    Orwell, *Homage to Catalonia*, pp 16–18

(b) The collectivisation of a Barcelona textile factory

By acclamation the workers decided to collectivise the factory.
. . . Meanwhile a workers' council had been set up and had taken
over the factory's management though leaving the former mana-
45 gers in their posts. One of the first steps taken was the abolition of
piece-work, an objective which the CNT textile unions had long
been fighting for.
    The first week, production fell by 40 per cent. We had calculated
that if it fell by no more than 25 per cent it would be possible to fix
50 a fair wage for all. But 40 per cent was impossible, it spelt the
collective's collapse. We called a general assembly, called on the
workers not to fail the collective attempts being made by the
Spanish proletariat to achieve social justice. For several weeks
production did not rise, we had to go round the shop floor,
55 haranguing the women workers. In the end they managed to get
production up to 70 per cent of its former level. . . .
    He noticed one big difference in the workforce after collectivisa-
tion. Prior to the war, none of the workers 'knew how to
talk'. . . . But the moment the factory was collectivised and there
60 were general assemblies everyone started to talk.
    It was amazing, everyone turned into a parrot, everyone wanted
to say what he or she thought and felt. They obviously felt
themselves in charge now and with the right to speak for
themselves.
    Andreu Capdevila, quoted in Fraser, *Blood of Spain*, pp 214–15

(c) Collectivisation and the war effort

65 At the end of October 1936 I went to the General Motors plant in
Barcelona (to obtain supplies of lorries for the army), and the
factory committee met to consider my request. I explained to them
that as the railway communications with Madrid were practically

cut, we were forced to provision Madrid by road and that we
70 therefore needed lorries. The committee gave me a sympathetic
hearing. . . .
'Don't worry comrade . . . the comrade who has just left has
gone to summon the foremen of the various workshops to arrange
shifts for mounting the chassis as soon as possible. We shan't stop
75 working till every single one of them is properly fitted up and
ready to go to Madrid.'
I returned to General Motors next day.
'Part of the work is finished and we have turned out thirty lorries
already, but we have some very unpleasant news for you . . .
80 Vallejo has forbidden the chassis to be mounted and said they must
not be sent to Madrid.'
'Who is Vallejo?'
'He is the secretary of the Barcelona War Industries Committee. . . . '
85 I found Vallejo seated at a desk full of telephones which were
constantly ringing. He sat there giving innumerable orders as
though he were a chief of staff. . . . 'You want us to put the
industries of Catalonia at the disposal of Madrid,' he said, 'and now
you want to take our lorries. But the Government refuses to grant
90 us foreign exchange which prevents us from buying raw materials
and coal and condemns our industries to unemployment. You
people in Madrid are idiotic enough to order your army uniforms
from the rickety industries in Valencia simply because you are
frightened of the revolution and don't want to come to terms with
95 us. . . . ' I told Vallejo that I did not accept his refusal and proposed
to attend the meeting of his committee that evening to talk about
my lorries. . . .
That night when I faced the committee I found them all waiting
for me with their claws out. . . . I explained that if Madrid fell,
100 Catalonia would be quite unable to complete its brilliant revolution
for the simple reason that it would not be allowed time . . . two
days later a hundred lorries had reached Valencia.

> J. M. Blazquez, *I Helped Build an Army* (London, Secker &
> Warburg, 1939), pp 167–70

(d) Catalan economic statistics 1936–1938

	Industrial production	Unemployment	Prices (1913 = 100)
Jan 36	100	55,288	169
June 36	98	72,782	172
Jan 37	70	91,416	224
June 37	68	79,404	304
Jan 38	60		434

> S. Payne, *The Spanish Revolution* (London, Weidenfeld &
> Nicolson, 1970), p 257

a   What do you understand by 'bourgeoisie' (line 33)?
b   Explain the reasons for the attacks by revolutionaries on the churches described in extract *a*.
c   Why did George Orwell regard the situation in Barcelona as 'worth fighting for'?
d   What advantages and disadvantages of collectivisation can be inferred from extracts *b* and *c*?
★ e   Why had rail communication with Madrid been 'practically cut' by October 1936?
f   Explain Vallejo's reluctance to supply lorries to Madrid.
★ g   What factors other than the effects of collectivisation might account for the figures given in extract *d*?
h   Of what value to the historian are statistical documents such as extract *d*?
i   'Had the spontaneous Revolution triumphed the war would soon have been lost' (Carr). Comment on this statement in the light of the evidence in the extracts.

2 The political dilemmas of the Republic

(a) The CNT enters Caballero's government, November 1936

The new Government was welcomed with great enthusiasm, particularly at the front. The very name of Senor Largo Caballero was enough to ensure its popularity. His splendid personal qualities, his scrupulous honesty and his tremendous capacity for
5   work were well known. . . .
      The gravest problems created by the encirclement of Madrid and the urgent necessity of avoiding internal disorders had decided him to bring the CNT into the Government, thereby forming a bloc of all the anti-fascist forces of the country. Senor Azana raised serious
10   objections however to the appointment of two of the four candidates proposed for the ministerial posts, Senora Montseny and Garcia Oliver, both members of the FAI. . . . In the dark days through which Madrid was passing any indecision would have been fatal. Already the proposed ministers, two of whom had come
15   expressly from Barcelona, had begun to suspect that their entry into the Government was not well-considered in high places and were talking about returning to Catalonia and breaking off negotiations. . . .
      A telephone conversation between the President of the Republic
20   and the Prime Minister, not lacking in a certain dramatic quality, put an end to an embarrassing situation. . . . Within a few moments Caballero was given authorisation to send to the official gazette the whole of the appointments of the four CNT members, duly sanctioned by the President. . . .

25   These new colleagues, with all the vehemence and heroics of the
Anarchist oratory, contended that the Government should stay in
Madrid and defend the capital in street-fighting at the barricades in
the manner of the Paris Commune. . . . Had the Anarchists not
been allowed to share the Government's responsibility it is more
30   than likely that they would have seized the opportunity afforded by
the Government's departure for Valencia to try to set up a local
Junta of their own.
    J.A. del Vayo (Socialist Foreign Minister in Caballero's
    Government), *Freedom's Battle* (London, Heinemann, 1940),
    pp 203–6

(b) Stalin's advice to Caballero, December 1936

Here are four pieces of friendly advice which we submit to you:
1. Attention should be paid to the peasants who are of great
35   importance in an agrarian country like Spain. It would be good to
issue decrees dealing with agrarian questions and taxation which
would meet the peasants' interests.
2. The urban petty and middle bourgeoisie must be attracted to the
Government side or at least given the possibility of taking up a
40   neutral attitude favourable to the Government by protecting them
against attempts at confiscation and issuing to them as far as
possible freedom of trade, otherwise these groups will follow
Fascism.
3. The leaders of the Republican Party should not be repulsed; on
45   the contrary they should be drawn in, brought close to the
government. . . . Above all it is necessary to ensure the Government the support of Azana and his group, doing everything
possible to help them overcome their hesitations. This is in order to
prevent the enemies of Spain from presenting it as a Communist
50   Republic and thus avert their open intervention which represents
the greatest danger to republican Spain.
Fraternal greetings,
K. Voroshilov, N. Molotov, J. Stalin (21 December 1936)
    J. Degras, *Soviet Documents on Foreign Policy, Vol 3, 1933–41*
    (Oxford, Oxford University Press, 1953), pp 229-31

(c) Dolores Ibarruri's speeches on the Revolution

(i) Speech made in August 1936

When we speak of Spain we mean not only the name, we mean a
55   democratic Spain, not the Spain which is clinging to her old
traditions; we mean a Spain which will give the peasants land,
which will socialise industry under the control of the workers,
which will introduce social insurance so that the workers may not

be condemned to a homeless old age; we mean a Spain which will
60 completely and comprehensively and in a new spirit, solve the
economic problems that lie at the foundation of all Revolutions.

On all fronts Communists, Anarchists, Socialists and Republicans
are fighting shoulder to shoulder. We have also been joined by non-
party people from town and country, because they too have
65 realised what a victory for fascism would mean for Spain.

> D. Ibarruri, *Speeches and Articles, 1936–38* (London, Lawrence
> & Wishart, 1938) pp 15–17, speech at Valencia 23 August
> 1936

(ii) Speech made in February 1937

From the earliest days of the fascist revolt the Communist Party
flung itself into the fight. . . . Unable to overcome the inertia of
those whose duty it was to create a regular army, we ourselves
proceeded to do so by forming the Fifth Regiment. . . . We need a
70 regular peoples' army. We need compulsory military training.
. . . We must give thought to the organisation of the munitions
industry. . . . Catalonia is the vital nerve of Spanish industry. . . .
Catalonia must feel that its ties with Spain are closer than ever and
Spain must help Catalonia with everything she needs. . . .
75   While there are elements in industry who are in a hurry for
socialisation, it must be confessed that so much discontent has
accumulated in the countryside that it may create a base for fascism
if we do not seriously tackle this problem. I am referring to the
attempts of the counter-revolutionary Trotskyite bandits, the
80 Franco agents, the 'uncontrolled elements' and certain anarchist
groups, to impose collectivisation in agriculture by force. . . . The
peasant loves the land and we always said that the Republic, the
revolution would give him land. But why force upon him a form
of husbandry he cannot understand and is not prepared for? . . .
85 One fine day some commission or other comes to this peasant
family and announces that it has no right to enjoy the fruits of its
labour because they belong to the collective. Comrades in plain
words that is robbery.

> Ibarruri, *Speeches and Articles,* p 53, speech in Barcelona, 3
> February 1937

(d) A POUM view

The cabinet of three Caballero men, three Prieto men, two
90 Stalinists, and five bourgeois ministers, which was established on
September 4, 1936, was a bourgeois government, a typical cabinet
of class collaboration. The classical social democrats of the Prieto
school could thus say, quite plainly, what the 'Spanish Lenin',
Caballero, and the ex-Leninists, the Stalintern, had to obscure: they

95　were currying favour with Anglo–French imperialism by strangling the revolution. . . . The question was sharply posed: either fight the non-intervention blockade and denounce Blum and the Soviet Union for backing it, or accept the Stalinist perspective of gradually winning away France and England from the blockade by demonstrating the

100　bourgeois respectability and stability of the Spanish Government. In other words, either accept the perspective of proletarian revolution and the necessity of arousing the international proletariat to aid Spain and spread the revolution to France, or accept class collaboration in Spain and abroad. When the alternatives became inescapable,

105　Caballero chose the latter. Within a few days, his comrade, Alvarez del Vayo, was off to grovel at the feet of the imperialists in the League of Nations.

　　　Caballero understood quite well that to arouse the Spanish masses to supreme efforts, it was necessary to offer them a programme of

110　social reconstruction. . . . To rouse the peasantry to struggle, to provide their best sons for the war, not as sullen, demoralised conscripts but as lion-hearted soldiers, to raise the food and fibres necessary to feed and clothe the army and the rear – that could only be done by giving the land to the peasantry. . . . Now the peasants and

115　agricultural workers had seized land . . . but still had no assurance that the government was not permitting it merely as a provisional measure for the war. . . . What the peasants wanted was a general decree nationalising the land throughout Spain.

　　　F. Morrow, *Revolution and Counter-Revolution in Spain* (London, New Park Publications, 1963), pp 47–50

Questions

★　*a*　In what circumstances had Caballero become Prime Minister in September 1936?

★　*b*　Who was Prieto (line 92) and what part did he play in the governments of Republican Spain?

★　*c*　What is meant in the context of the extracts by 'the Paris Commune' (line 28); 'petty and middle bourgeoisie' (line 38); 'Trotskyite bandits' (line 79); 'Stalintern' (line 94); 'class collaboration' (line 92); 'Anglo-French Imperialism' (line 95).

　　d　Why were Caballero and his colleagues eager to include members of the CNT in the cabinet? Why would Azana object to their inclusion?

　　e　In what ways does extract *a* suggest that del Vayo was biased against the CNT?

　　f　To what extent does extract *b* support the view that Stalin was more interested in the security of the Soviet Union than in promoting a revolution in Spain?

　　g　To what extent had Dolores Ibarruri changed her political views between the dates of her two speeches in extract *c*?

h On what points does Dolores Ibarruri's second speech agree
with the advice offered by Stalin in extract *b*?

★ *i* Explain the reference to 'grovelling at the feet of the Imperialists
in the League of Nations' (lines 106–7). How powerful was the
League by the end of 1936?

j What do the language and content of extract *d* indicate of the
political sympathies of the writer?

k How effectively does Morrow in extract *d* rebut the arguments
in extract *b* and *c*(ii)?

3 Soviet influence in the Republic

(a) A novelist's view of Soviet influence

He had not liked Gaylord's, the hotel in Madrid the Russians had
taken over, when he first went there because it seemed too
luxurious and the food too good for a besieged city and the talk too
cynical for a war. . . . Gaylord's was the place where you met
5 famous peasant and worker Spanish commanders who had sprung
to arms from the people at the start of the war without any
previous military training and found that many of them spoke
Russian. . . .

It was at Gaylord's that you learned that Valentin Gonzalez,
10 called El Campesino or the Peasant, had never been a peasant but
was an ex-sergeant in the Spanish Foreign Legion who had deserted
and fought with Abd el Krim. . . . That was alright. . . . Why
shouldn't he be? . . . You had to have these peasant leaders quickly
in this sort of war. . . . You couldn't wait for the real Peasant
15 leader to arrive and he might have too many peasant characteristics
when he did. So you had to manufacture one. . . .

At Gaylord's too you met the simple stonemason, Enrique Lister
from Galicia, who now commanded a division and who talked
Russian too. And you met the cabinet worker, Juan Modesto from
20 Andalusia who had just been given an army corps. . . . He was the
most trusted of the young soldiers by the Russians because he was a
true party man. . . . Lister's and Modesto's and Campesino's
troops had all fought well in the battle of Guadalajara. . . . But
Lister and Campesino and Modesto had been told many of the
25 moves they should make by their Russian military advisers. They
were like students flying a machine with dual controls which the
pilot could take over whenever they made a mistake. . . . I wonder
how Lister will be once the dual controls are gone. But maybe they
won't go he thought. I wonder if they will go? Or whether they
30 will strengthen? I wonder what the Russian stand is on the whole
business?

E. Hemingway. *For Whom the Bell Tolls* (London, Penguin,
1955), pp 219–25

(b) A Soviet adviser returns to Russia in February 1937

'I'm going to take you to a party', Koltsov [the Pravda correspondent in Madrid] said and seized me by the hand.

He led me into a room where a dozen high officers of the
35 delegation were assembled clad in civilian clothes. Gorkin, an engineer, was the first to greet me. He had set up searchlight installations for us, the only defence we possessed against night air-attacks. . . . Now he had been recalled to Russia and this was his farewell party. He was beaming with satisfaction. His work had
40 been approved of and in Moscow he would get his reward. . . . A waiter filled our glasses with champagne and Maximovich [the leader of the Russian delegation], toasted Gorkin in a little speech which moved him to tears. . . .

The next day Koltsov . . . found me on the balcony of the staff
45 building. Pointing to the searchlight beside me he asked, 'What's that?'

'A legacy from Gorkin' I replied still in the best of spirits.

He laughed cuttingly and said 'A legacy? That's the literal truth!'

'Has something happened to him on his journey?' I asked.
50 'No', said Koltsov, 'on the journey? No. But something will happen to him when he arrives. . . . He'll be arrested when he reaches Odessa.'

For some moments I was dumbfounded. Then I asked: 'How do you know? Is it something political?'
55 'Yes', said Koltsov, 'why are you so surprised? Because of his farewell party? We all knew about it. In fact that's why we gave him a party. It's why Maximovich came.'

I was feeling slightly giddy. I moved nearer to the balustrade at the edge of the balcony. . . .
60 'I'm going into the line', I said, 'I don't feel well.'

'It's not easy for a European to get used to Asiatic customs,' said Koltsov.

'I prefer American customs', I said, 'I'm going to join Hemingway. One can breathe more freely in his neighbourhood if you'll forgive
65 my saying so.'

'I'll come with you', said Koltsov and he muttered as he straightened his revolver-belt, 'perhaps I need a breath of western democracy too!'

> G. Regler, *The Owl of Minerva* (London, Rupert Hart Davis, 1959), pp 294–6. Regler was a German Communist who fought in Spain.

Questions

a   What may be inferred from extract *a* about the extent of Soviet influence in Republican Spain?

b   Of what value to a historian is the extract from Hemingway's novel? How does it differ from the type of evidence offered in extract *b*?

* *c* To what developments in Russia in the mid-1930s does extract *b* refer?

4 Civil War within the Civil War in May 1937

(a) George Orwell on the May Days in Barcelona

It will never be possible to get a completely accurate and unbiased account of the Barcelona fighting, because the necessary records do not exist. Future historians will have nothing to go upon except a mass of accusations and party propaganda. I myself have little data
5 beyond what I saw with my own eyes and what I have learned from other eyewitnesses whom I believe to be reliable. . . .

First of all what actually happened? . . . On May 3 the Government decided to take over the Telephone Exchange which had been operated since the beginning of the war mainly by CNT workers; it
10 was alleged that it was badly run and that official calls were being tapped. Salas the Chief of Police sent three lorry loads of armed civil guards to seize the building. . . . At about the same time bands of Civil Guards seized various other buildings in strategic spots. . . . There was a widespread belief that this was the signal
15 for a general attack on the CNT by the Civil guards and the PSUC. The word flew round the town that the workers' buildings were being attacked, armed Anarchists appeared on the streets, work ceased and fighting broke out immediately.

That night and next morning barricades were built all over the
20 town, and there was no break in the fighting until the morning of 6 May.

The fighting was, however, mainly defensive on both sides.
. . . Roughly speaking the CNT-FAI-POUM forces held the working class suburbs and the armed police forces and the PSUC
25 held the central and official portion of the town . . . [on 7 May] people began to leave the barricades of their own accord. . . . The official leaders of the CNT had joined with those of the UGT in imploring everyone to go back to work. . . . By the afternoon of 7 May conditions were almost normal. That evening 6000 Assault
30 Guards sent by sea from Valencia arrived and took control of the town. . . .

My own opinion is that the fighting was only preconcerted in the sense that everyone expected it. . . . On the Anarchist side the action was almost certainly spontaneous for it was an affair mainly
35 of the rank and file. . . . The Friends of Durruti distributed some kind of revolutionary leaflet but this did not appear until 5 May and cannot be said to have started the fighting. . . . The official leaders of the CNT disowned the whole affair from the start. . . . The fact

that the CNT was still represented in the Government and the
40   Generalitat ensured that its leaders would be more conservative
than their followers . . . the main object of the CNT leaders was to
form an alliance with the UGT.

   The POUM leaders did not disown the affair . . . but in reality
the attitude of the POUM leaders was hesitating. They had never
45   been in favour of insurrection until the war against Franco was won
. . . in spite of issuing revolutionary slogans about the 'reawaken-
ing of the spirit of 19 July' . . . they did their best to limit the
workers' action to the defensive. *La Batalla* also issued instructions
that no troops should leave the front.

   Orwell, *Homage to Catalonia,* pp 141–5

(b) The Daily Worker's *account of the Barcelona fighting*

50   The German and Italian agents who poured into Barcelona
ostensibly to 'prepare' the notorious 'Conference of the Fourth
International' had one big task. It was this: They were – in co-
operation with the local Trotskyists – to prepare a situation of
disorder and bloodshed, in which it would be possible for the
55   Germans and Italians to declare that they were 'unable to exercise
naval control of the Catalan coasts effectively because of the
disorder prevailing in Barcelona' and were, therefore, 'unable to do
otherwise than land forces in Barcelona.' The instrument for all this
lay ready to hand for the Germans and Italians in the shape of the
60   Trotskyist organisation known as the POUM.

   The POUM, acting in co-operation with well-known criminal
elements and with certain other deluded persons in the Anarchist
organisations planned, organised and led the attack in the rear-
guard, accurately timed to coincide with the attack on the front at
65   Bilbao. . . .

   Daily Worker, 11 May 1937

Questions

a   Who were the 'Friends of Durruti' (line 35)?
b   What is meant by the PSUC (line 15) and Fourth International
(lines 51–2)?
c   Why according to extract *a* did the official leaders of the CNT
and the POUM not support the rising?
d   In what ways does extract *a* contradict the view of the May
Days given in extract *b*? Which account do you find most
convincing?
e   What is meant by 'party propaganda' (line 4)? How might
extract *b* be described as 'party propaganda'?
★ f   What changes occurred in Republican Spain as a result of the
May Days?

5 A historian's assessment of Negrin's government

Much has been made of the 'counter-revolutionary' nature of
Negrin's government and its subservience to Communist directives. Its declared purpose was to create a strong war government
'to unify the command of military operations as well as the control
5 of economic life'. . . . Negrin was a man of considerable charm
and enormous energy. . . . He has been violently attacked, especially by anti-Communists and ex-Communists, as at best a
bourgeois politician . . . at worst a mere tool of the Soviet Union
via the Spanish party. . . . All the new government's measures –
10 strict censorship, the tightening-up measures against spies and
political dissidents, the prohibition of criticism of the only foreign
ally – can be regarded as either the normal measures of a war-time
government or as support for a ruthless Communist campaign
against political opponents. . . .
15   Negrin's policies rested on two axioms: firstly that sooner or
later France and Great Britain would have to come out against the
dictators and help Spain. . . . Secondly that, until this happened,
nothing could be done that would offend the Soviet Union to the
point where it would refuse arms supplies. This implied a working
20 alliance with the Communist party, without sacrificing every
democratic principle to the demands of the party machine. It was a
delicate and dangerous balancing act.
  R. Carr, *The Spanish Tragedy, the Civil War in Perspective*
  (London, Weidenfeld & Nicolson, 1977), pp 197–8

Questions

 a What, according to this extract, were Negrin's relations with
   the Spanish Communist Party and with the Soviet Union?
★ *b* How likely was it given the foreign policies of these two
   countries in 1937 that France and Britain would eventually aid
   the Republic?
★ *c* How successful was Negrin in imposing political unity in
   Republican Spain?

6 Life in Republican Spain

(a) An American writer describes life in besieged Madrid in April 1937

I wake up suddenly with my throat stiff. It's not quite day. I am
lying in a comfortable bed in a clean well-arranged hotel room
staring at the light indigo oblong of the window opposite. I sit up
in bed. Again there's the hasty loudening shriek, the cracking roar,
5 the rattle of tiles and a tinkling shatter of glass and granite
fragments. Must have been near because the hotel shook. . . .

It's funny how the least Spanish building in Madrid, the proud New York baroque tower of Wall Street's International Tel and Tel, the symbol of the colonising power of the dollar, has become
10 in the minds of the madrilenos the symbol of the defence of the city. Five months of intermittent shellfire have done remarkably little damage. . . .

Inside you feel remarkably safe. The whole apparatus of the telephone service still goes on in the darkened offices. The elevators
15 run. It feels like Sunday in a New York downtown building. In the big quiet office you find the press censors, a cadaverous Spaniard and a plump little pleasant voiced Austrian woman. . . . It's not surprising that the censor is a nervous man; he looks underslept and underfed. He talks as if he understood, without taking too much
20 personal pleasure in it, the importance of his position of guardian of those telephones that are the link with countries technically at peace, where the war is still carried on with gold credits on bankledgers and munitions contracts and conversations on red plush sofas in diplomatic anterooms instead of with six-inch shells
25 and firing squads. . . .

It's a relief to get away from the switchboards of power and walk out in the sunny streets again. If you follow the Gran Via beyond the Plaza de Callao down the hill towards the North Station stopping for a second in an excellent bookshop that's still open for
30 business, you run into your first defence barricade. It is solidly built of cemented paving stones laid in regular courses high as your head. That's where men will make a last stand and die if the Fascists break through. . . .

Up another little hill is the burned shell of the Montana Barracks
35 where the people of Madrid crushed the military revolt last July. Then we're looking down the broad street of the Paseo de Rosales. It used to be one of the pleasantest places in Madrid to live. . . . Now it's no-man's land. The lines cross the valley below, but if you step out on the paseo you're in full view of the enemy on the
40 hills opposite and the Moors are uncommonly good riflemen.

John dos Passos quoted in Cunningham (ed.), *Spanish Front, Writers on the Civil War*, pp 119–122

(b) A journalist describes the position of women in Republican Spain

I remember sitting in a cafe at night, with . . . Calero the barrister and the second-in-command of the International column . . . Serna, the lame lawyer and district judge was there too. . . .

I remember we were talking about the new marriage laws and
45 the status of women under the revolution . . . Calero said 'People are marrying like flies in summer. It's quite easy, you can marry whoever you like without giving notice, and it only takes five

minutes all told. No formality.'

He showed us a marriage certificate form. When I read it I was
delighted that our Andres Nin was Minister of Justice and had done
it all. There was a paragraph in it addressed to the husband which
said: 'You are asked to remember that your wife goes into marriage
as your companion, with the same rights and privileges as
yourself.'

It added that women were equal to men, that the revolution had
restored them to their natural place in society and could admit of no
sex domination. . . .

I asked Serna: 'What do you think of that?'

'I think it's fine. Especially here. Women were barbarously
treated before.'

'Well, why do you leave your wife shut up just as you did
before? I never see her out with you.'

He was furiously indignant and stamped his walking stick on the
ground, his black eyes snapping.

'What on earth do you mean? Of course she comes out with me.
It's not at all the same as before. Why I take her to the cinema at
least twice a week!'

I realised then how hard the old mould was to crack in spite of
the best good will. . . .

'And the divorce?' I asked.

'That only takes five minutes too, and it's quite easy.'

'What grounds do you admit?'

'Oh, the wife has all the same permitted reasons for divorcing
her husband as he had for divorcing her. Besides that, if two people
come to us and want to divorce and seem determined about it, we
don't see any reason for muddling their lives for them. We don't
prevent them from having a fresh start'. . . .

The Spanish women were anxious to grab their liberty, but they
had been closed up and corsetted so long that they didn't know
how much of it there was to be had. Often they were content with
the little scraps which answered their first call. It seemed so much
to them. . . . The religious heritage was very hard to get rid of.
The family was another thing. Louise Gomez . . . decided to build
a women's secretariat in the party [the POUM], and form a
women's regiment and women's classes and lectures and centres of
education and child welfare. She received more than 500 adherents
within the first week . . . but dozens of full-blown matrons and
young girls confided to me:

.'Of course I wasn't able to tell my husband (or my father) that I
was coming here, he would have had a fit. I just had to say I was
joining a sewing-circle.'

Mary Low and Juan Brea, *Red Spanish Notebook* (San
Francisco, City Lights Books, 1979), pp 179–86. (First
edition 1937)

(c) Standards of living

(i) Bilbao in February 1937

Although the fighting was far away, the town was near starvation,
Meat, milk, eggs, butter were completely unobtainable. Breakfast,
lunch and dinner were indistinguishable as all consisted of rice and
95 garbauza beans. In the cafes you could buy thick, sweet, black
chocolate served in cups accompanied by slices of greyish bread.
Half-starved children crowded round the cafe patrons begging for a
spoonful of chocolate or a piece of bread.

J. Mitford, *Hons and Rebels* (London, Gollancz, 1977), p 121

(ii) Rations in the Republic (figures in grams per day

	1936	1937	1938
100 Bread	700	600	400
Meat or fresh fish	250	200	150
Fresh vegetables	200	250	180
Butter and fat	60	60	50

Payne, *Spanish Revolution,* p 358

Questions

a   Explain the sentence 'the war is still carried on with gold credits
. . . diplomatic ante-rooms' (lines 22–4).

b   Who was 'Andreas Nin' (line 50) and what eventually became
of him?

★   c   Using extract *b* and your own knowledge explain how and why
the Civil War had changed the position of women.

d   What factors according to extract *b* prevented women achieving
full equality in Republican Spain?

e   To what extent is Jessica Mitford's account in extract *c*
supported by the figures in the table?

★   f   Explain the shortage of food in Republican Spain.

VI Nationalist Spain

Introduction

All those on the Republican side in the war regarded themselves as fighting against fascism and this view prevailed among the supporters of the Republic long afterwards. However, historians have recently begun to examine Franco's regime more critically and they have generally concluded that it owed more to Spanish military traditions than to Hitler or Mussolini.

The nature of Franco's regime is one of the most interesting controversies of the war. Was it a fascist regime analogous to that of Mussolini or an old-style military dictatorship dominated by a 'non-Falangist Franco' (Blinkhorn)? A lot depends on how fascism is defined, on Franco's own views, the extent to which he controlled, or was controlled by, the Falange and his relationship with the German and Italian governments.

Franco's accession to power owed much to chance (the deaths of his rivals, Jose Antonio and Generals Sanjurjo, Goded, Fanjul and later Mola), and also his command of the vital Army of Africa. When Mola set up his Defence Junta in Burgos in July 1936 it was not clear what form of government Nationalist Spain would acquire. However, it was agreed that a unified command was essential and in September 1936 Franco became Head of State.

According to Carsten he 'had no intention of adopting the revolutionary slogans and demands of the Falange with which he was entirely out of sympathy. He was a conservative of the old school, and his revolt a putsch by army leaders, not a social and national revolution.' Spanish fascism had emerged in 1931 with the Juntas de Ofensive Nacional Sindicalista (JONS) which merged with Jose Antonio's Falange in 1934. The Falange at the beginning of 1936 had less than 10,000 members, although, like the Communists in the Republican zone, it became a mass movement with its own militia after the rising. It was, however, hampered by the imprisonment of Jose Antonio and it was only one of several elements in the rebellion. Faction fighting broke out in the Falange in April 1937 between supporters and opponents of its new working-class leader Hedilla. This gave Franco his opportunity to merge it under his own leadership with the only other mass popular force, the Carlists, into a new political party.

The Falange provided Franco and his influential brother-in-law Serrano Suner with an ideological framework for his new state. There were some fascist overtones, notably in the Labour Charter which paid lip-service to the corporate state, but the Falange was not allowed much political initiative and was firmly subordinated to the army.

Franco's politics were mainly characterised by a hatred of liberal democracy and of political parties which he considered had ruined Spain in the years before the Civil War. Certainly his title of Caudillo echoed those of Führer and Duce. However, the Germans and Italians, to their frustration, as the extracts in this chapter show, never gained the influence over Franco and his policies which they hoped for, though a holding company, HISMA-ROWAK, was quickly established to operate the export of Spanish ores and raw materials to Germany. Franco was much more adroit than his counterparts in the Republic in avoiding foreign control. Fascist trimmings concealed what many historians agree was basically an old-style military regime, 'a re-creation of the regime of the Catholic kings' (Carr).

It can still be argued that the Spanish right before 1936 and Franco's regime after that date, shared with Italian fascism 'antagonism towards democracy and the left and a common commitment to some sort of authoritarian corporate state' (Blinkhorn). However, Franco's regime only partly fits the definition of fascism as 'a movement seeking the fullest possible control over all aspects of life by means of a single-party system'. Franco was 'authoritarian rather than totalitarian' and in most respects his regime looked back rather than forward. The government was dominated by Conservative monarchists and a powerful position was accorded to the Catholic Church. Much less was done than in Germany or Italy to change the economic order or to establish any totalitarian control over economic or social life.

Whatever differences of opinion there may be over the character of Nationalist Spain, there is general agreement that the political unity imposed by Franco must be counted as a major reason for the Nationalist victory.

1 Franco becomes Head of State

(a) Decree agreed by the generals at Salamanca, 29 September 1936

Article 1 All Land, Sea and Air forces that collaborate or will collaborate in future with the Movement shall be subordinated to a single command, which should be filled by a divisional general or a vice-admiral.

5   Article 2 The man named will be styled Generalissimo and will
     have the highest place in the military hierarchy, military and naval
     officers of the highest rank being subordinate to him.
     Article 3 The post of Generalissimo will be combined with an
     office of Chief of State for the duration of the war and, in the latter
10   capacity, his authority will extend over all national activities:
     political, economic, social, cultural etc.
     Article 3 aroused instant and noisy disapproval (among the generals
     present). . . .
          Crozier, *Franco*, p 212

(b) Decree signed by General Cabanellas, Chairman of the National Defence Committee at Burgos, 30 September 1936

     Article 1 In fulfilment of the agreement adopted by the National
15   Defence Committee, His Excellency Don Francisco Franco Baha-
     monde has been appointed Head of the Government of the Spanish
     State and will assume all the powers of the New State.
     Article 2 He is likewise appointed Generalissimo of the National
     Land, Sea and Air Forces, and the post of Chief General of the
20   Operational Armies is conferred upon him.
          Crozier, *Franco*, p 213

(c) Nationalist radio broadcast, 1 October 1936

     ATTENTION! ATTENTION!
     Tonight in a memorable broadcast from Radio Castilla you are
     going to hear the authentic voice of Spain in the plenitude of its
     power. . . . The voice of the Caudillo, the chief, the guide, the
25   maximum figure of the Spanish state. Spaniards and foreigners,
     General Franco is going to speak. Viva Franco! Viva Franco! Viva
     Espana!
          Fraser, *Blood of Spain*, p 201

Questions

★   *a*   How had Franco managed to become the most important figure
          in Nationalist Spain by the end of September 1936?
    b   Why would some of the generals disapprove of Article 3 of
          extract *a*?
    c   What is the significance of the differences in the wording of the
          decrees in extracts *a* and *b*?
★   *d*   What were the German and Italian equivalents of the title of
          Caudillo (line 24)?
    e   How effectively does the style and content of extract *c* portray
          Franco's position as the supreme leader of Nationalist Spain?

2 Political conflicts in Nationalist Spain

(a) An American journalist comments on divisions in Nationalist Spain

Franco's propaganda had drawn much attention to the strange companions who were fighting side by side under the Republican flag . . . but I found in Salamanca that the discords in the Franco ranks were just as deep and bitter. From one end of Nationalist
5 territory to the other there were two predominant uniforms: one was the Carlists with their khaki shirts and bright red berets and the other the Fascists (or Falangists), in navy blue with crimson tassels swinging from their caps. These two groups . . . though bound together by a common detestation of parliamentary government,
10 held views stubbornly and bitterly opposed. The Carlist party . . . wanted nothing less than a return to the feudal system. With these reactionary views they considered the Falangists a dangerous and radical organisation.

I heard Carlists argue that the peasant should stay on the clod of
15 land on which he was born; that his happiness did not lie in education but in the security that the great landowner could give him. A Falangist leader commenting on these views, shook his head emphatically, 'that is the way they talk,' he said, 'but when the war is over there won't be any great landowners . . . '.
20 Count Florida said vehemently that half the Fascists were nothing but Reds. . . .

> Virginia Cowles, *Looking for Trouble* (London, Hamish Hamilton, 1941) pp 78–80

(b) A Falangist's view

It was only in the second phase of Jose Antonio Primo de Rivera's thinking that syndicalism had been mentioned as a form of self-management of the economy. . . . In this phase, Jose Antonio was
25 striving to go beyond Mussolini-type fascism of a corporative state modelled on Catholic thinking, to discover a form in which traditional Spanish utopian syndicalism could be used to collectivise the economy. I understood his thinking to mean that the economy must be run by a vast federation of trade unions
30 representing the different branches of production which would lead to self-managing industries within a planned economy. . . .

After Franco took over there was an outright capitulation and we had to accept two unions, one for management, the other for workers, within the national-syndicalist structure. This duality,
35 with the important role allotted to union bureaucrats, portended little more than what in fact happened: the Franquista vertical trade unions. We spoke like fascists, saluted like fascists, wore fascist uniforms and aspired to fascist ideals. At the same time we believed

that fascism as it existed was an excessively limited type of
40 nationalist reaction to the situation which had arisen from the end
of the First World War, and was not a sufficiently substantive
doctrine to become the third force between an outworn liberalism
and an unacceptable Marxism. . . .

[In the Falange] you could be a revolutionary and still be a
45 conservative, a nonconformist and a conformist. There was no
need to reject your traditional upbringing, especially nationalism.
Indeed the latter formed part of the new equation: the diminished
state of Spanish society, the poverty of large sectors of its
inhabitants went hand in hand with the loss of Spain's power as a
50 nation. . . . Only an enlightened minority can transform the
country; a proletarian revolution destroys the traditional elements
of a society, cuts the latter off from its own history. Only territorial
expansion can provide the conditions which will produce general
prosperity . . . thus reducing class differences and finally eliminat-
55 ing the class struggle. . . .

Falangists like myself with more ideological commitment began
to favour the entry of left-wingers into the movement. Within the
nationalist camp, the Falange after all represented the most left-
wing posture possible. . . . Cases of left-wingers joining became
60 so notorious that the right called the Falange the FAIlange. Firstly
because our flag was the same red and black; secondly because of
our pseudo-revolutionary demagogy, and lastly because we
accepted everyone. . . .

What I didn't see then was that the military . . . would be
65 influenced by the old conservative forces so that the war would end
with all our efforts negated and the wealthy classes dominating
again.

> Dionisio Ridruejo quoted in Fraser, *Blood of Spain,* pp 313–16

(c) Nationalist propaganda posters (see page 92)

Questions

a Explain what is meant in the context of the extract by
'syndicalism' (line 27); 'corporative state' (line 25); 'outworn
liberalism' (line 42).
b Why would the Falangists be called the 'FAIlange' (line 60)?
c What did the writer of extract *a* consider to be the main
differences between the Carlists and the Falange?
★ d What effect had Jose Antonio's death in November 1936 had on
the leadership and development of the Falange?
e What evidence is there in extract *b* to support the views in
extract *a* that the Falange were 'a dangerous and radical
organisation' and that 'half the Fascists were nothing but Reds'?

(a) Nationalist propaganda posters

92   THE SPANISH CIVIL WAR

f What did the author of extract *b* consider should be the main characteristics of Spanish fascism?

g What impression of Franco's regime is conveyed by the posters in extract *c*? How effective are these posters as Nationalist propaganda?

h How far do extracts *b* and *c* support the view that Franco's policies were not fascist?

3 Franco takes over the Falange, April 1937

(a) The German Ambassador reports a conversation with Franco, in April 1937

On 11 April I had a conversation with General Franco lasting more than two hours in the course of which he expressed his views on some questions of domestic policy, the future form of government and the military situation. . . . The Falange which in its ideas
5 leaned heavily on the National Socialists and Fascist model had only a year ago been very weak numerically. Only after the beginning of the Nationalist movement led by Franco, had the Falange with considerable assistance from nationalist-minded officers, obtained a great number of adherents and thereby its
10 present importance. But after the death of Jose Antonio Primo de Rivera, regarding whose death there is in Franco's opinion no doubt, the Falange lacked a real leader. Young Primo de Rivera, although he had as yet had little experience, had been a leader because of his intelligence and energy. His successor Hedilla was a
15 completely honest person, but by no means equal to the demands imposed on the leader of the Falange. . . .

As for the leaders of the monarchist parties, Franco spoke against Fal Conde in particular. He had not so long ago taken a number of measures for the reintroduction of the monarchy which he, Franco,
20 could not but regard as directed against him and the Government. He had therefore summoned the most prominent leaders of the Requetes, who had told him that they in no way approved of Fal Conde's conduct. . . .

Regarding his attitude to the Falange and the monarchist parties
25 Franco told me that he wishes to fuse these groups into one party the leadership of which he himself would assume. To my objection that the leadership of a party would take up a very great deal of his time . . . Franco replied that he, as head of the new unity party intended to form a Junta, probably consisting of four members of
30 the Falange and two representatives of the monarchist groups. The core of the unity party would be formed by the Falange which had the soundest programme and the greatest following in the country.

I discussed this development yesterday with our *Landesgruppen-*

leiter and the representative of the Fascio at the Italian Embassy; the
35 latter, not inaccurately, described the situation in these words:
'Franco is a leader without a party, the Falange a party without a
leader.' If in his attempt to bring the parties together Franco should
meet with opposition from the Falange, we and the Italians are
agreed that, in spite of all our inclination toward the Falange and its
40 sound tendencies, we must support Franco, who after all intends to
make the programme of the Falange the basis of his internal policy.
The realisation of the most urgently needed social reforms is
possible only with Franco, not in opposition to him.

I then directed the conversation with Franco to the rumour
45 which had been circulating here for several weeks regarding an
impending regency . . . Franco told me that for Spain the return of
the monarchy was absolutely out of the question for the foreseeable
future. . . . He would consider it wrong however to adopt
measures . . . which were calculated to block the road to a
50 monarchy at a later date. Only after the completion of the
reconstruction of Spain, which would take a long time, could one
consider whether a certain continuity could not be established by a
reintroduction of the monarchy.

Documents on German Foreign Policy, Vol 3, p 267

(b) Franco's call for unification, 19 April 1937

In Spain as in other countries where there are totalitarian regimes,
55 traditional forces are now beginning to integrate themselves with
the new forces. The Falange Espanola has attracted masses of
young people by its programme, its new-style propaganda, and
had provided a new political and heroic framework for the present
and a promise of Spanish fulfillment in the future. The Requetes, in
60 addition to possessing martial qualities, have served through the
centuries as the sacred repository of Spanish tradition and of
Catholic spirituality, which have been the principal formative
elements in our nationality. . . .

Because of all the foregoing,
65 I order that:
Article 1: The Falange Espanola and the Requetes, together with
all their existing services and units, shall be integrated, under my
leadership, into a single entity of national character which
henceforth shall be named the Falange Espanola Tradicionalista y
70 de las JONS. All other political organisations and parties are hereby
dissolved.
Article 2: The guiding organs of the new national political entity
shall be the Chief of State (*Jefe del Estado*), a Secretariat or Political
Junta and the National Council. . . .
75 Half of the members (of the Secretariat) will be designated by the

Chief of State; the other half will be elected by the National
Council. . . .
Article 3: The fighting forces of the Falange Espanola and of the
Requetes shall be fused into a single National Militia. . . .
80 The National Militia shall serve as an auxilary of the Army.
The Chief of State shall be the Supreme Commander of the
Militia. . . .

> C. F. Delzell (ed.), *Mediterranean Fascism* (New York,
> Harper & Row, 1970), pp 294–5

Questions

★   *a*   How accurate was the view that the 'Falange had leaned heavily
on the National Socialist and Fascist model' (line 5)?
★   *b*   What developments within the Falange provided Franco with
an opportunity to take control of it in April 1937?
★   *c*   What 'measures for the reintroduction of the monarchy' (line
19), had been taken by Fal Conde?
d   Comment upon the skill with which Franco in extract *a*
persuaded the German Ambassador to support his political
plans.
e   How did the decree quoted in extract *b* succeed in keeping
power in Franco's hands?

4 The British government's representative in Spain describes Franco's first government

On 30 January 1938 the Secretariat-General of State in Salamanca
was dissolved and a Cabinet on normal lines established in Burgos
in its place. It was composed of eleven Ministers, Franco remaining
President and continuing to hold supreme command of the Land,
5   Sea and Air Forces, while General Count Gomez Jordana, besides
being Minister for Foreign Affairs, was Vice-President of the
Government. . . . An ardent Monarchist, a patriotic Spaniard and
a convinced Liberal, the idea that Spain had had to have recourse to
German and Italian aid was, of course, revolting to him and only
10 excusable in view of its dire necessity. . . . To a Spaniard of his
way of thinking, to whom a restoration of the Monarchy provided
the only future for Spain as he envisaged it, the establishment of the
Nationalist Government could at best be but a temporary
expedient. . . .
15 Jordana's fellow Ministers were half Traditionalist, half Falange,
General Martinez Anido, who had been a valuable supporter of
Alfonso XIII and a right-hand man to the Dictator, being Minister
of Public Order and Ramon Serrano Suner, Minister of the Interior
. . . it was soon obvious that [Suner] was destined to be a

20   prominent figure in the administration. In the first place he was the
Caudillo's brother-in-law, which had won for him the nickname of
'Cunadisimo' or 'Super-brother-in-law'. Secondly he had been a
close friend of Jose Antonio, founder of the Falange. . . . Other
prominent figures were the Conde de Rodezno, who for many
25   years had been head of the Traditionalist Party and was appointed
Minister of Justice, and Fernandez Cuesta who, since 1934, had
been National Secretary of the Falange and became Minister of
Agriculture.

        Sir R. Hodgson (British agent to the Nationalist Govern-
ment for November 1937) *Spain Resurgent* (London, Hutch-
inson, 1953), pp 89, 109–10, 117

Questions

a   What evidence is there in the extract to support the view that
Franco's government was not mainly fascist?

b   Why would Jordana have been eager to convince Hodgson of
the views expressed in lines 8–14?

c   What do you deduce from this extract of Hodgson's opinions of
Franco's regime?

5 German and Italian influence in Nationalist Spain

(a) Mussolini discusses Spain with Ribbentrop, November 1937

We want Nationalist Spain, which has been saved by virtue of all
manner of Italian and German aid, to remain closely associated
with our manoeuvres. . . . Rome and Berlin must therefore keep
in close contact so as to act in such a way that Franco will always
5   follow our policy. Franco has given proof of possessing qualities
remarkable in a Spaniard. He is calm, discreet, a man of few words.
Towards us he has maintained an attitude of lively sympathy.
However there is no denying that he is already feeling certain
negative influences such as that of the great landowners and upper
10   clergy. . . .

    Turning to the attitude of Franco the Duce affirms that he must
necessarily remain attached to our political system, first because
our pressure will prevent him breaking away and also because his
ideology being close to ours, he has taken a path from which he
15   will not be able to retreat. . . .

    First he must adhere to the Anti-Comintern Pact. Second, we
will make a Tripartite Pact, whereby Franco will undertake to
bring Spanish policy into line with that of the Rome–Berlin Axis.

        Muggeridge (ed.), *Ciano's Diplomatic Papers,* pp 144–5

(b) The progress of the German-Spanish mining project, January 1938

We were not making any progress in the Montana affair. The
20 matter had now been pending for two months. Senor Sangroniz
explained that the matter was important from the point of view of
principle and that the present provisional Spanish Government had
to be exceptionally careful with regard to its disposition of the
Spanish patrimony. . . . Germany brought up mines and mining
25 rights to an incredible extent. This of course aroused opposition
everywhere and the Spanish Government was forced to settle the
matter fundamentally on the basis of Spanish law.

> *Documents On German Foreign Policy, vol 1.* pp 569–70; memo
> from German Ambassador to the Foreign Office, 26 January
> 1938

(c) A press correspondent's view in August 1937

German and Italian flags flew from one end of Spain to the other.
. . . I was not prepared for such an open flaunting of the Fascist
30 alliance. In Salamanca . . . hotels, bars and restaurants blazed with
swastikas and the colours of Savoy. . . . The Gran Hotel was
decorated with posters of the dictators . . . the scene of the hotel
lobby was a cosmopolitan one. German colonels sat solemnly
drinking café au lait, while Spanish general staff officers with bright
35 blue sashes round their waists, strode importantly across the
marble floor. Italians booted and spurred, usually with a girl on
each arm, came jingling down the stairs. . . . It was difficult to get
rooms at the Gran Hotel and most of the rooms were occupied by
Germans. The top floor was used as a German HQ and guarded by
40 the guardia civile. . . .
    Needless to say the internal affairs of Spain were being carefully
manipulated by the Nazis. . . . Most important of all was the
German infiltration into almost all the departments of State
administration. Through their influence they were able to see that
45 Fascist sympathisers secured important bureaucratic jobs, thus
establishing key men throughout the fabric of government.

> Cowles, *Looking for Trouble*, pp 68–80

Questions

★ *a* What were the Anti-Comintern Pact (line 16), and the Rome-
Berlin Axis (line 18)? Why would the German and Italian
governments wish Spain to join these agreements?

★ *b* How accurate was Mussolini's statement that Nationalist Spain
had 'been saved by virtue of all manner of German and Italian
aid' (lines 1–2)?

★ *c* Explain the reference to the 'colours of Savoy' (line 31).

d Why did Mussolini consider the influence of the great land-owners and the upper clergy on Franco to be 'negative' (line 9)?

★ *e* Why did Germany need Spanish minerals?

f How cleverly in extract *b* did Sangroniz argue against German control of Spanish mines?

g How much proof does Virgina Cowles produce in extract *c* to substantiate her view that the 'internal affairs of Spain were being carefully manipulated by the Nazis'? To what extent is her view at variance with the evidence in extracts *a* and *b*?

★ *h* Franco was described by the German Ambassador as a 'clerical reactionary'. How accurate is this description of his political views?

6 The condition of the working class in Nationalist Spain

(a) Economic improvements in Andalusia

General Quiepo de Llano ran the nationalist zone of Andalusia and Estremadura like a viceroyalty. . . . He set out to introduce a regime which assured the 'harmonious co-existence of capital and labour'.

5 'I ask you workers, does disorder, anarchy and gangsterism suit you better than a government which imposes freedom from above? The real freedom, which ends where that of your neighbour begins?' he asked in a speech at the opening of a building site for cheap workers' housing. . . .

10 He promised that no great fortunes would be made in future while people were dying of hunger. As a gesture of intent, he forbade employers to sack workers without 'prior authorisation from the regional labour office'; and abolished employers' associations, for 'it is not fair that workers' organisations should disappear

15 while employers have associations to defend their interests, interests which must be abolished'.

Convinced that the major part of the ills which afflicted Spain originated in its 'abandoned state of agriculture', he set in motion a number of projects. One of these was to drain and put into

20 cultivation 100,000 hectares of the marshlands along the Guadal-quivir from Seville to the sea to provide work and homes for several thousand families. . . . 'With the result that an area where hardly any rice was grown before has become the most important rice-growing area of Spain. . . '.

25 [In 1937] a cotton-processing industry was launched with a capitalisation of 100 million pesetas. Difficulties in getting foreign exchange out of the Burgos administration to buy machinery in

Switzerland . . . were overcome with Queipo's help. . . . Raw cotton prices were fixed for the farmer – calculated on equivalent guaranteed prices for maize and chick-peas – and the prices of finished textile products were also regulated. . . .
30

Fraser, *Blood of Spain*, pp 277–8

(b) The Labour Charter, March 1938

Reviving the Catholic tradition of social justice and the lofty sense of humanity that inspired the laws of the Empire, the State, which is national by reason of being an instrument at the service of the
35 entire Nation and syndical in so far as it represents a reaction against nineteenth century capitalism and communistic materialism, embarks upon the task of carrying out . . . the revolution that Spain is achieving to ensure that Spaniards may once more possess for good and all, their Country, Bread and Justice. . . .
40 I   Work for all.
All Spaniards have the right to work. The satisfaction of this right is one of the main concerns of the State. . . .
II   Hours and conditions of work.
The State undertakes to exercise constant and effective action in
45 defence of the worker, his living and his work. It will set proper limits to the working hours to prevent them being excessive and will grant labour every safeguard of a defensive and humanitarian order. It will specially prohibit night work for women and children, regulate homework and free married women from the
50 workshop and the factory. . . .
Every worker will have the right to paid yearly holidays in order to enjoy a deserved rest, and the necessary machinery to ensure the better fulfillment of this order will be prepared. . . .
III   Remuneration and security.
55 The minimum basis of payment for work shall be sufficient to provide the worker and his family with a worthy, moral living.
Family subsidies will be established through suitable bodies.
The standard of living of the workers will be raised gradually and inflexibly in proportion as the higher interests of the nation
60 permit. . . .
X   Social insurance
Savings will give the worker the certitude of being protected when in misfortune.
There will be an increase in the social insurances against old age,
65 disablement, maternity, work accidents, . . . and unemployment, the ultimate aim being the establishment of total insurance. A primary aim will be to devise means for providing a sufficient pension for superannuated workers. . . .
VIII   Capital and its role.
70 The head of the Firm will take on himself its management, and be

responsible to the State for the same. . . .

After allotting a fair interest to capital, the profits of the Firm will be firstly applied to the reserves necessary for its sound position, the improvement of production and the betterment of working
75   conditions and the living of the workers. . . .

XI   Protection and production.

Individual or collective acts that in any way disturb normal production or attempt to do so, will be considered as crimes of treason against the Country. . . .
80   Unjustifiable slackening in output will be the subject of appropriate punishment. . . .

XIII   Principles of the Organisation.

All factors of economy will be incorporated, by branches of production or services in vertical Guilds. . . .
85   The vertical Guild of a corporation by public law, which is formed by combining into one single organism all elements that devote themselves to fulfilling the economic process with a certain service or branch of production, arranged in order of rank, under the direction of the State.
90   The officials of the Guilds will necessarily be chosen from the active members of the Falange.

     Delzell (ed.), *Mediterranean Fascism,* pp 305–11

(c) *Daily life in Burgos*

The huge number of persons who have been shot or imprisoned, the practice of denunciation, encouraged and in some cases, forced upon people, the hysterical behaviour of the priests and continued
95   incitement to violence, – all this has brought a helpless people into an indescribable condition of bewilderment and fright. The wage-earning classes in particular, in the power of relentless employers, who by a well-prepared stroke have got them now at their mercy, are going through a crisis of despondency and acute distress. The
100 people in desperation is seeking protection in such organisations as still subsist in Nationalist territory, which explains the remarkable headway made by the Falangists.

     Vilaplana, *Burgos Justice,* p 229. (Vilaplana became an opponent of the Nationalists and fled to France in June 1937)

Questions

a   What do you understand by 'materialism' (line 36)?

b   What reasons does extract *c* give for the workers joining the Falangist organisations?

c   What does extract *b* infer about the intended role of women in Nationalist Spain?

d   How might extract *b* be used both to support and to disprove the view that the terms of the Labour Charter were favourable to Spanish workers?

e   In what ways does extract *c* contradict the statements in extract *b*?

f   In what ways could you use these extracts to support the argument that Nationalist Spain was both Paternalist and Totalitarian?

★ *g*   What similarities are there between the economic policies described in the extracts and those already introduced by Mussolini and Hitler into Italy and Germany?

h   How far do the extracts support the view that Spain was achieving a 'revolution' (line 37)?

7 Life in Nationalist Spain

(a) Women

(i) The Margaritas of Talfalla,
Solemnly promise on the Sacred Heart of Jesus,
1. To observe modesty in dress: long sleeves, high necks, skirts to the ankle, blouses full at the chest.
5   2. To read no novels, newspapers or magazines, to go to no cinema or theatre, without ecclesiastical licence.
3. Neither publicly nor in private to dance dances of this century but to study and learn the old dances of Navarre and Spain.
4. Not to wear makeup as long as the war lasts.
10   Long live Christ the King! Long live Spain!
          Quoted in Fraser, *Blood of Spain*, p 309

(ii) With all its blemishes, Falange had unquestionably, its virtues. I was most favourably impressed by the work done by Pilar, 'The Absent One's' sister and head of the Women's Section . . . created in 1936 in Valladolid by the widow of Don Onesimo Redondo, a
15   fervent Falangist [the Auxilio Social] was run most competently by women . . . who in their blue uniforms and white aprons, unquestionably rendered a real service to a country plunged into the miseries of Civil War. A year after its creation, it already had 711 centres for feeding children. Two years later the number was
20   quadrupled, while millions of hot meals were served in them. Also destitute adults were fed . . . and innumerable meals distributed for home consumption. Another branch had workshops where warm clothes were made for the destitute, while aid for mothers and children was provided in the shape of creches, schools and the
25   like. . . . When on 26 January 1939, Barcelona fell and a starving population looked forward in despair to the continuation of its

misery as the certain sequel, Auxilio Social by its assistance, distributed to the motto: 'Franco's justice brings food for all', did most useful propaganda work.

Hodgson, *Spain Resurgent*, pp 93–4

(b) The Press Law, April 1938

30   Article 1: The State is responsible for the organisation, supervision and control of the national institution of the periodic press. . . .
Article 2: In the exercise of this function, the State shall:
1. Regulate the number and extent of periodical publications.
2. Intervene in the naming of the managerial personnel.
35   3. Regulate the profession of journalism.
4. Supervise the activity of the press.
5. Have the power of censorship. . . .
Article 8: The director of each periodical bears responsibility for it. He must be inscribed in the Official Register of Publishers . . . and
40   to hold his position he must have the approval of the Ministry. . . .
Article 10: In the case of a signed article, the responsibility of the signer in no way exempts the director of the periodical from responsibility for publishing the article.
Article 20: The punishments for directors and enterprises to be
45   decreed by the Ministry of the Interior may range . . . among the following:
(a) Imposition of a fine.
(b) Dismissal of the director.
(c) Dismissal of the director, accompanied by the cancellation of
50   his name in the Register of Publishers.
(d) Confiscation of the periodical. . . .
I decree the present Law, in Burgos, this 22nd day of April, 1938, the Second Triumphal Year.
The Minister of the Interior,
55   Ramon Serrano Suner.

Delzell (ed.), *Mediterranean Fascism*, pp 312–13

(c) A day in the life of a Nationalist pilot in San Sebastian

8.30. Breakfast with the family.
9.30. Take-off for the front; bombard enemy batteries; machine-gun convoys and trenches.
11.00. Rudimentary golf in the club at Lasarte, next to airport and
60   partially usable.
12.30. Sun-bathing on the Ondarreta beach and quick splash in the calm sea.
13.30. Shellfish, beer and a chat in a cafe in the Avenue.
14.00. Lunch at home.
65   15.00. Short siesta.

16.00. Second sortie, similar to this morning's.

18.30. Cinema. Old, but wonderful movie, with Katherine Hepburn.

21.00. Aperitif in the Bar Basque. Good Scotch, animated atmos-
70 phere.

22.15. Dinner at the Nicolasa Restaurant, war songs, camaraderie, enthusiasm.

> Quoted in Preston, *The Spanish Civil War*, pp 116–18

Questions

a   Explain the reference to 'the Absent One' (lines 12–13).

b   Why is extract *b* dated 'the second triumphal year' (line 53)?

c   To what extent do the two extracts in *a* offer contradictory views of the role of women in Nationalist Spain?

d   Using extract *a* and the extracts on women in chapter V compare the position of women in Nationalist and Republican Spain.

e   What does extract *b* reveal of the methods by which Franco's government kept control of the press?

f   In what ways does extract *c* imply that life in San Sebastian was largely unaffected by the war?

★ g   What influence did the Catholic Church acquire over life in Nationalist Spain?

VII Nationalist Success, April 1937 to March 1939

Introduction

In spring 1937 Franco abandoned the seige of Madrid in order to concentrate on the conquest of the North. The campaign was to be notorious for the destruction of the Basque cultural centre, Guernica, by the Condor Legion, responsibility for which was denied by the Nationalists for many years afterwards.

The Nationalist capture of the North is generally recognised to have been a decisive turning point in the war, depriving the Republic of a powerful industrial base and of 25 per cent of its armed forces. Republican attempts to divert the Nationalist armies with offensives at Brunete and Belchite in the summer of 1937 all failed.

In December 1937 the Republicans attacked the town of Teruel, a weakly held sector of the front near Madrid. But initial success turned to disaster and the Republican armies collapsed, enabling Franco's troops to advance rapidly towards the Mediterranean. On 15 April 1938 Nationalist forces reached the sea, cutting the Republican zone in half. From this point Negrin's government had no policy except survival, hoping that the European situation would change in their favour. However, the failure of a final desperate offensive across the Ebro and British and French appeasement of the Dictators at Munich dashed Republican hopes. In January 1939 Franco swiftly conquered Catalonia and the Republic disintegrated in political faction fights. Early in March Colonel Casado carried out a successful coup against the Communists in Madrid but shortly afterwards was forced to agree to unconditional surrender. On 30 March 1939 the Nationalists entered Madrid and on 1 April the war was officially over.

The reasons for the Nationalist success have been widely debated by historians. Understandably emphasis has been placed, especially by supporters of the Republic, on the greater amount of foreign aid received by Franco enabling the Nationalists to achieve crucial air superiority with new models of German and Italian aircraft by mid-1937: 'Franco could not have won the Civil War without the unstinting aid of Hitler and Mussolini' (Paul Preston). Hugh Thomas considers the timing of aid and German willingness to supply it at crucial moments, for example for the advance into Aragon in 1938 and for the final campaigns of the war, and without political strings, to have been more important than the quality of the material. Some historians argue that what is surprising is not the defeat of the Republic but the fact that it held out so long against overwhelming odds.

Raymond Carr considers that 'it was less aid than the moral unity and logistic superiority of the Nationalists which was decisive in the long run'. A major reason for the Republican's defeat was their inability to sustain and follow through offensives. While the Republicans were often successful in defence they consistently failed to gain territory or to make decisive breakthroughs. The responsibility for these failures is difficult to ascribe. Was it due to political disunity or simply to deficient military tactics and to 'the lack of junior commanders to carry through the impetus of its initial élan' (Alpert)? Whatever the reason, by April 1939 the future of Spain for the next forty years had been determined.

1 The destruction of Guernica

(a) An eyewitness account

I arrived at Guernica on April 26th at 4.40pm. I had hardly left the car when the bombardment began. The people were terrified. They fled, abandoning their livestock in the market place. The bombardment lasted until 7.45. During that time five minutes did not elapse
5   without the skies being black with German planes. The planes descended very low, the machine gun fire tearing up the woods and roads, in whose gutters huddled together, lay old men, women and children. Before long it was impossible to see as far as 500 yards owing to the heavy smoke. Fire enveloped the whole city. . . . As
10 a Catholic priest I state that no worse outrage could be inflicted on religion than the Te Deum to be sung to the glory of Franco in the church at Guernica which was miraculously saved by the heroism of the firemen from Bilbao.

> Father Albert Onaindia, a Basque priest, quoted in Preston,
> *The Spanish Civil War*, p 140

(b) A British journalist's account

Guernica, the most ancient town of the Basques and the centre of
15 their cultural tradition, was completely destroyed yesterday after-noon by insurgent raiders. The bombardment of this open town far behind the lines occupied precisely three hours and a quarter,

during which a powerful fleet of aeroplanes consisting of three
German types, a Junkers and Heinkel bombers, and Heinkel
20   fighters, did not cease in unloading on the town bombs weighing
from 1000 lb downwards and it was calculated more than 3000 two
pounder aluminium incendiary projectiles. The fighters meanwhile
plunged low from above the centre of the town to machine gun
those of the civilian population who had taken refuge in the fields.
  G. L. Steer (who arrived in Guernica on the night of 26
  April) in *The Times*, 28 April 1937

(c) *A German squadron leader remembers*

25   The first squadron dropped their bombs. I saw them, but by the
time I was over the target, the town was obscured by dust and
smoke, so we had to drop our bombs as best we could . . . we
couldn't tell what they were hitting. . . .
  Hans Henning quoted in G. Thomas and M. Morgan, *The
  Day Guernica Died* (London, Hodder & Stoughton, 1975),
  preface

(d) *Evidence from an American journalist*

We arrived [in August 1937] in Guernica to find it a lonely chaos of
30   timber and brick. . . . There were only three or four people
standing in the streets. One old man was standing inside an
apartment house that had four sides to it but an interior that was
only a sea of bricks. . . . Accompanied by Rosalles [a Nationalist
press officer], I went up to him and asked if he had been in the town
35   during the destruction. He nodded his head and when I asked him
what had happened waved his arms in the air and declared that the
sky had been black with planes, 'Aviones', he said, 'Italianas y
Alemanes'. Rosalles was astonished. 'Guernica was burned', he
contradicted heatedly. The old man however stuck to his point,
40   insisting that after a four hour bombardment there was little left to
burn. Rosalles moved me away. 'He is a Red,' he explained
indignantly.
  Later [in Santander] Roselles described to Nationalist staff
officers the incident at Guernica. 'They tried to tell us it was
45   bombed not burnt.' The tall staff officer replied, 'But, of course it
was bombed. We bombed it and bombed it and bombed it and
bueno, why not?'
  Rosalles looked astonished and when we were back in the car
again heading for Bilbao he said, 'I don't think I would write about
50   that if I were you.'
  Cowles, *Looking for Trouble*, pp 71–5

(e) A Nationalist account

During the advance on Bilbao Guernica became part of the front
line. Even before this happened the town was a military objective.
It contained several small factories, one of them engaged in the
manufacture of arms and ammunition. It was an important road
55 junction . . . and a depot of substantial size for the massing of
reserves on their way to the trenches, or for sheltering combatants
after a spell of duty in the lines. . . .

The Republicans in Bilbao needed a sensational story to offset
their reverses. They dispatched Asturian miners to dynamite
60 Guernica and set fire to its buildings and swore that they had been
blown to smithereens by German bombs. Partly bombarded
previously for sound reasons . . . evidence of havoc was not
wanting. . . . The report that the town and its inhabitants had been
destroyed by German bombs was invented for propaganda
65 reasons. . . .

To destroy an entire small town . . . not hundreds but
thousands of bombs would be required. The resources for such
wholesale destruction are entirely lacking to either side in this war.
Apart altogether from the question of expediency, such destruction
70 would mean using a month's supply of ammunition for General
Franco's entire army and denuding all fronts of air protection to
indulge in an orgy of lunatic folly. . . . Mr. G.L. Steer's blood-
curdling accounts to London were partly responsible for the world
circulation of the myth. . . .

75 It should be noted that the destruction though involving many
buildings spared the Guernica Tree and adjoining structure. Basque
separatists took great care not to damage the Tree which they held
in special veneration. . . . A dispatch from the Army of the North
[not intended for publication] in 28 April 1937 states, 'Basque
80 fugitives who had reached our lines were terrified by the tragedies
enacted in such towns as Guernica, deliberately burnt and
destroyed by the Reds while we were not more than ten miles
away. There is much indignation among our troops against the
Basque-Soviet leaders who blame Nationalist aviators for these
85 barbarous acts. Our planes during the last few days were unable to
fly due to persistent fog and drizzle. . . .

Bolin, *Spain, the Vital Years*, pp 274–8, 357

(f) Another Nationalist view

I learned something about the famous Guernica controversy
through my friendship with a British and a French journalist who
entered the town with the first Nationalist troops to occupy it, and
90 who closely examined the damage and questioned many of the
inhabitants. This was the communists' most successful propaganda

coup of the war, and it created a myth which, fostered by the skill of Agitprop and immortalised by the genius of Picasso, has passed into history.

P. Kemp, in P. Toynbee (ed.), *The Distant Drum*, p 71

Questions

a   Explain the references to 'the Guernica Tree' (line 76); 'Basque separatists' (lines 76–7); 'agitprop' (line 93); 'immortalised by the genius of Picasso' (line 93).

★   b   Why did the Basque clergy not share the Spanish Church's support of the Nationalists?

c   How far do the accounts in extracts a and b corroborate one another?

d   The German pilot quoted in extract c was interviewed in 1974. With what caution might a historian approach his evidence?

e   How convincing is Luis Bolin's explanation of the destruction of Guernica in extract e?

f   Which version of the destruction of Guernica is most substantiated by extract d?

g   Which of these sources might a historian be most likely to trust and why?

2 Franco's northern campaign

(a) Map of the division of Spain in March 1937 (p 109)

(b) A Basque view of the war in the north

Of course militarily there should have been a single command. But there was no understanding between us and the others – the Asturians and the people from Santander. We found it very hard to feel Spanish. Whether one likes it or not, that's the truth. . . . The
5   iron ring [defences round Bilbao] was virtually useless anyway. The Socialist turner . . . found that the concrete pill-boxes were not camouflaged and the trenches were wide and straight. We had no confidence in it. . . .

We could have held the enemy off . . . but it required a war
10   policy of the sort that the Basque government was unlikely to carry out. A scorched earth policy, a revolutionary type of war like in Madrid.

Quoted in Fraser, *Blood of Spain,* pp 396–404

(c) The German Ambassador's view of the war, July 1937

The capture of Bilbao signifies not only a military and a great moral victory but also possession of one of the most important harbours

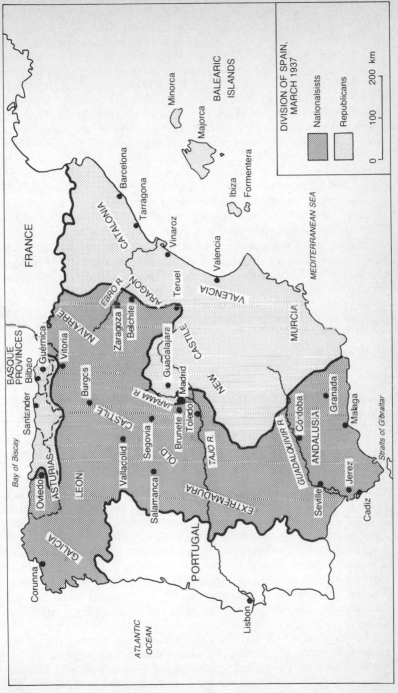

(a) Spain in March 1937

15   in Spain and above all, of the iron ore mines which are extremely
valuable for the manufacture of war materials and ammunition. . . .

    The disproportionately long duration of the operations against
Bilbao is due in part to the differences of opinion between Franco
and the Italian General Doria. . . . It is a noteworthy fact that with
20   regard to the direction of operations the Generalissimo
undoubtedly feels relieved by the death of General Mola. He told
me recently, 'Mola was a stubborn fellow and when I gave him
directions which differed from his own proposals he often asked
me, "don't you trust my leadership any more?"' . . .
25   The advance west of Madrid and other local attacks by the Reds
prove that the hope of their early moral collapse, already voiced on
occasion, was premature. Even if Franco succeeds in quickly
holding the attack west of Madrid, which is probably directed by
General Miaja, and then resumes the offensive against Santander,
30   the enemy there nevertheless has at least gained time to bring up
new equipment and ammunition, to improve training of his troops
and to build fortifications. . . . The probablilty of a victorious
conclusion of the war before the end of the year becomes
considerably less than heretofore.

> The German Ambassador in Salamanca to the Foreign
> Ministry, 9 July 1937, *Documents on German Foreign Policy*,
> pp 409–10

(d) Dolores Ibarurri describes the Brunete and Belchite offensives

35   All the North fell into the hands of the rebels – men, iron, steel,
minerals, coal, wood, heavy industry, precision arms, explosives,
electrical power plants, meat, milk, hides, fruit, fish. . . . The
Republic was losing its territory and bleeding to death.

    As a diversionary manoeuvre the Central General Staff organised
40   an offensive against the rebel troops in Brunete in July 1937 and
later on the Aragon front. . . . It was chiefly the men of the Fifth
Regiment who carried out the Republican offensive in Brunete.
They were already a part of the Peoples' Army organised by
Negrin and they brought discipline, fighting spirit and organisation
45   to its ranks. Lister and Modesto had the task of putting the General
Staff's plan into practice and they did it brilliantly. Had it not been
for the sabotage of their operations by Colonel Casado and
company they could have destroyed the entire enemy front in
Madrid.
50   The Peoples' Army swiftly won Brunete but had no chance to
put this advantage to use. The army was forced to hold out in
Brunete, by now converted into ruins, for almost a month. Enemy
aviation bombed the town day and night. Republican forces were
powerless to stop the raids partly because of their lack of aviation,

55 but chiefly because the General Staff sabotaged the entire operation. . . .
    It was an agonising sight to watch one wave of enemy airplanes
after another raid our positions, wipe out our units and inflict
terrible losses on that legion of heroes. After four long weeks of
60 resistance without water, without most necessary supplies and
without reserves to relieve the combatants, the order was given to
abandon Brunete.
    One month later in another diversionary movement, the General
Staff decided to start a series of operations in Aragon in the
65 direction of Saragossa. The operations were planned by Comrade
Cordon, a professional soldier and member of the Communist
Party, dedicated heart and soul to the cause of the people. . . .
    After a brief rest, the troops that had fought in Brunete were sent
to the Aragon front to carry out the planned offensive. The
70 Republic could not rely on the undisciplined FAI militia, much less
on the Anarchist militia of Ascaso to carry out such an important
mission.
    With the arrival of Lister's troops in Caspe, the FAI's reign in
that region of Aragon came to an end. Republican order was
75 established. The Anarchist Ascaso went to France, later to
America, taking with him the booty he had extracted from his
experiments in 'libertarian communism'. . . .
    The Aragon offensive could have been started many months
earlier had it not been for the policy of tolerance towards the
80 military inactivity of the Anarchist militia. The offensive compelled the fascist commanders to withdraw their forces from other
fronts and concentrate them in Belchite to contain the advance of
the Peoples' Army. While this operation, too late, too limited,
failed to prevent the fall of the North, it was at least proof that
85 something had changed in the new government's concepts of
waging the war, and that the Peoples' Army was able to handle
successfully offensive as well as defensive operations.
        D. Ibarruri, *They Shall Not Pass* (London, Lawrence &
        Wishart, 1966), pp 296–9

Questions

 a Compare the map in extract *a* with the map in chapter II of
    Spain in August 1936. In what respects had the positions of the
    Nationalists and Republicans altered between August 1936 and
    March 1937?
 b What light does extract *b* throw on the reasons for the
    Republican defeat in the North?
 c What do extracts *a, c* and *d* reveal of the advantages to the
    Nationalists of the capture of the northern coast of Spain?

d   Why do you think Franco was relieved by Mola's death (line 21)?
e   What was the purpose of the Republican offensives described in extracts *c* and *d*?
★   f   Do you consider the German Ambassador's estimate of the Nationalist position to have been unduly pessimistic?
g   'Plagued by continual factional disputes over strategy, tactics and supply, the Republicans proved unable to recapture lost territory' (Martin Blinkhorn). Comment on this view in the light of the evidence in extract *d*.

3 Non-intervention; the Nyon Conference, September 1937

(a) Churchill's letter to Eden on the eve of the Nyon Conference, September 1937

This is the moment to rally Italy to her international duty. Submarine piracy in the Mediterranean and the sinking of ships of many countries without any care for the lives of their crews must be suppressed. . . . In these routes the French and British Navies
5   should search for all submarines and any found by the detector apparatus should be pursued and sunk as pirates. Italy should be asked in the most courteous manner to participate in this. If however she will not do so, she should be told 'that is what we are going to do'. . . .
10   It is not believed that Germany is ready for a major war this year, and if it is hoped to have good relations with Italy in the future, matters should be brought to a head now. The danger from which we suffer is that Mussolini thinks all can be carried off by bluff and bullying, and that in the end we shall only blether and withdraw. It
15   is in the interests of European peace that a firm front should be shown now. . . .
Speaking personally I feel that this is as important a moment for you as when you insisted upon the Staff conversations with France after the violation of the Rhineland. The bold path is the path of
20   safety.
> W. Churchill, *The Second World War,* Vol 1, *The Gathering Storm* (London, Cassell, 1967), pp 220–1

(b) Ciano gives the Italian view of Nyon

September 3: Full orchestra – France, Russia, Britain. The theme – piracy in the Mediterranean. Guilty – the Fascists. The Duce is very calm. He looks in the direction of London and he doesn't believe the English want a collision with us.

25   September 13: Ingram and Blondel [the British and French diplomats in Rome], have given us a copy of the Nyon decision. I have prepared a reply in which, without advancing a claim to take part, I affirm our right to parity. It will certainly embarrass them. Either we co-operate or the scheme fails and they are to blame. I am
30   awaiting for approval from Berlin before delivering any reply.
   September 21: Blondel and Ingram handed me a note which gives us virtual satisfaction though the word parity is carefully avoided. The Duce has approved my reply and the press communique. . . . It is a fine victory. From suspected pirates to policemen of the
35   Mediterranean – and the Russians, whose ships we were sinking, excluded!
           Ciano's Diaries 1937–38 (London, Methuen, 1952), pp 8–15

Questions

★   *a*   What is meant by the 'violation of the Rhineland' (line 19) and why had it resulted in Staff conversations with the French?
★   *b*   Explain the reference to 'piracy in the Mediterranean' (line 22). How was this issue resolved at the Nyon Conference?
★   *c*   What grounds did the Duce have for believing that Britain did not desire a collision with Italy in 1937 (lines 24–5)? What developments in Anglo-Italian relations had taken place by the end of the Spanish Civil War?
    d   To what extent does Ciano's account of the crisis substantiate Churchill's fear that Britain might 'only blether and withdraw'?

4 Nationalist triumphs in 1938

(a) A German gunner in the Condor Legion describes the Nationalist advance towards the Mediterranean in spring 1938

From the meandering front lines on our maps of Aragon, pencilled arrows sprout towards the Mediterranean, indicating the progress of the March offensive, destined to split Republican Spain in two. In the path of the advancing columns lies the town of Belchite, its
5   first objective. . . .
   I cannot help marvelling at our own vast superiority in numbers and material. Streams of Heinkel 111s, protected by Messerschmitt fighters and alternating with Italian Caproni and Savoia bombers, carry out their missions unopposed but for the occasional twin
10   puffs of smoke from the enemy's double-barrelled French anti-aircraft guns. Some four miles away the mountains resemble erupting volcanoes from heavy Nationalist gunfire. . . .
   We never have to worry about the supply of ammunition. . . . The long barrels of our guns are like pointers indicating the
15   progress of battle. The higher the elevation, the farther the enemy

has been driven back. . . . 'The village of Fuendetodos has fallen. For tonight expect Liberty!' Message received. Cheers go up. . . . According to the map, the advance must have covered close to twenty miles. After the stalemate at Teruel during the recent winter campaign, this is quite extraordinary. . . . We do not pitch tents but prepare to huddle together for a few hours sleep on the stony ground. . . . Some bloody Spaniards come tearing along in lorries, exuberantly singing their hymn 'Face towards the Sun', with headlights appropriately on full beam. Foot soldiers arrive and set bonfires ablaze. Attracted by the commotion it does not take long for our nocturnal visitor to appear.

It is an enemy spotter and nuisance plane. We call him the 'Red Ghost', for nobody has ever seen him, or simply the 'coffee-grinder' because of the obsolete sound of the engine. He has soon spotted us in the clear moonlight. For the first time I hear the hiss of falling bombs, soon to become familiar to city-dwellers all over Europe. We dive for cover in the blinding flash of explosions, but the result is negative. . . .

> Alfred Lent, 'The blond Moors are coming' in Toynbee (ed.), *The Distant Drum*, pp 99–101

(b) An interview with the Republic's Foreign Minister in May 1938

In late May 1938 I saw Alvarez del Vayo, Minister of Foreign Affairs, in Paris in a little hotel on the left bank. He radiated energy, confidence, enthusiasm. Sitting on the edge of his chair and leaning forward, his pugnacious protruding chin thrust out, his eyes kindling, he spoke vigorously in English with his peculiar German accent.

As usual he was in a fighting mood. Knowing him personally before he was minister I plied him with impertinent questions without fear of his resentment and I am sure he replied with candour. True, he admitted the time had been when stout Catalan resistance could not have been counted upon. But a great change had come over the Catalans. The barbarous massacre of women and children had aroused a fighting spirit. . . .

'But the division of your territory . . . ' I began.

'That was foreseen', he broke in, 'and provisions have been made. The Government can fight on for a year and Madrid can last that long.'

With that he handed me a document of great length, a list of all the food ships that had reached Barcelona, Tarragona, Valencia . . . from 1 December to 1 May, 'that for Franco's blockade', he said grimly.

> C. Bowers, *My Mission in Spain* (Gollancz, London, 1954), pp 382–3. (Bowers was the American Ambassador to Republican Spain but was based in France mainly in St Jean de Luz during the war).

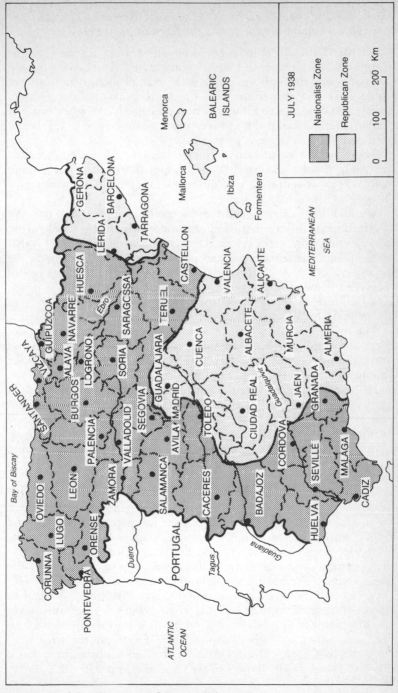

(*c*) Map of the division of Spain, July 1938

(d) A medical worker in the International Brigades describes the Republican counter-attack across the Ebro in July 1938

55　We crossed the Ebro by night, one night after the first of the troops. With Crome and his Adjutant, we drove down steep hairpin bends through the dusty dark, but all along the route we could hear and sometimes see, the local peasants laying down swathes of branches to fill up the potholes and hacking away at the
60　rocky sides to make the corners more manoeuvrable for heavy vehicles. We just made it by dawn. . . .

There were a lot of casualties; an avalanche of work descended with which we could barely cope (though I still went on making tea) and for an agonising few moments every day I scrutinised for
65　George's [her husband], name.

We had daily air raids and were sometimes under shell fire. An illustration of the terrible handicap under which the whole army was fighting (due to the criminal policy of non-intervention) is that when planes came over we had no need to identify them as the
70　enemy or 'ours'. A glance at the sky was enough. If it was one of ours, the sky was full of bursts of anti-aircraft fire, while if it was one or more of theirs – and they often came in formation – an occasional puff of smoke was all that could be seen. . . .

The bridges across which all our supplies reached us were under
75　incessant bomb attacks. Sometimes all of them were damaged and could not be repaired for hours or as much as two days, though the fortification units slaved heroically. . . .

Its first onslaught over, the 15th Brigade got a few days rest. I visited the British Battalion, a raggle-taggle bunch of weary men,
80　scattered over an arid hillside. George was there, unharmed. . . . I was taken to see Sam Wild, the Commander of the Battalion. Dear, gruff old Sam's first greeting was, ''Ave you etten?' (pure Lancashire hospitality). He told me that George had been 'mentioned in despatches'.

85　They went back into the lines, where the British won the name of the 'Shock Battalion' for its part in the near successful attack upon Hill 481 outside Gandesa. But the long, slow, desperate and heroic retreat of the Spanish People's Army battling against the overpowering superiority of the Fascists, aided by German and
90　Italian troops and war material in growing force, had begun. We lost ground. There were a few hours when our hospital and HQ were actually between our own and the enemy lines. We had to retire quickly, back towards the river where we set up in yet another derelict farmhouse, not far from a railway tunnel which
95　had been converted into a hospital, for safety from the air.

Nan Green, 'Death on the Ebro', in Cunningham (ed.),
Spanish Front, Writers on the Civil War, pp 235–7

Questions

★ *a* Explain the references to: the hymn 'Face towards the Sun' (line 23); 'falling bombs soon to become familiar to city dwellers all over Europe' (lines 31–2); 'Franco's blockade' (line 53).

★ *b* Explain the reference to the 'stalemate at Teruel' (line 19).

★ *c* Why did the Republican Government decide to launch the Ebro offensive?

d What reasons do extracts *a* and *d* provide to explain the Nationalists' success and how far can this success be attributed to foreign assistance?

e How convincing do you find Del Vayo's assessment of the position of the Republic in extract *b*?

f Using the map in extract *c* explain why by the summer of 1938 it appeared unlikely that the Republicans could win the war.

5 The dilemmas of foreign powers

(a) The Blum government considers ways and means of helping Republican Spain, 15 March 1938

The permanent committee of national defence held its eleventh session on 15 March 1938 under the presidency of M. Edouard Daladier, Minister of National Defence and of War.

The subject of the session was the study of the following questions:

5 1. Aid for Czechoslovakia in the event of German aggression.

2. Intervention in Spain. . . .

M. Leon Blum, Prime Minister, introduced the second question that he wanted to put to the Comité Permanent: How can we intervene in Spain? How can we support an ultimatum to General

10 Franco of this kind: 'If within 24 hours you have not renounced the help of foreign troops France . . . will take whatever measures . . . she judges necessary . . . ?' It would, he observed, be a manoeuvre of the same kind as that which Chancellor Hitler had just tried . . . in Austria and carried out.

15 General Gamelin, Chief of National Defence Staff, remarked that the conditions were not the same. We normally had an active army of 400,000 men in France while the Germans had 90,000 men. . . .

M. Campinichi, Minister for the Navy, asked what in view of the weakness of our air force would be the effect on the war of

20 Germany's air supremacy?

General Vuillemin, Chief of Air Staff, considered that in 15 days our air force would be crushed. . . .

M. E. Daladier, Minister of National Defence and War, declared

that one would have to be blind not to see that intervention in Spain
would unleash a general war. It did not seem possible to intervene
except in the event of a new factor: important foreign reinforcements. . . .

> Quoted in Adamthwaite, *The Making of the Second World
> War*, pp 181–2

(b) Cartoon, October 1938

EUROPE'S AUCTIONEER
"——And, of course, this one for you, Sir."

(c) The Soviet Union begins to withdraw

Stalin's slogan 'stay out of range of the artillery fire', became more
insistent after Japan's invasion of China and threat to the Siberian
frontier. . . . Gradually during 1938 Stalin withdrew his hand
from Spain. All he got out of the adventure was a pile of Spanish
gold.

> Krivitsky, *I Was Stalin's Agent*, p 134

Questions

★ a What manoeuvre had Hitler just carried out in Austria (lines
13–14)?
  b To what extent is it true to say that extract *a* is 'permeated with
defeatism'?

★   *c*   Who is the figure in the cartoon handing over Spain and Czechoslovakia? In what circumstances had Hitler obtained Czechoslovakia?

      d   What do you deduce from extract *b* of the cartoonist's opinions of the foreign policy of the British government?

★   *e*   Why has it been said that Munich was 'a death-blow to the hopes of the Republic'?

★   *f*   What was the significance for the Soviet Union of the Japanese invasion of China (line 29)? What other reasons might Stalin have had for withdrawal from Spain?

★   *g*   Was Krivitsky correct in his statement that Stalin had gained nothing except Spanish gold from his adventure in Spain?

6 The end of the War

(a) Colonel Casado describes Negrin's conference with his military commanders at Albacete on 26 February 1939

The Prime Minister told us he thought the situation very serious but that circumstances made it imperative for us to continue the war. He said that the problems of catering and transport could be solved. As for armaments, apart from the war material which was
5 in France as a result of the retreat from Catalonia, there were large quantities of machine guns, batteries and aeroplanes, all acquired by the Government in other countries and that probably all these arms could be brought to Spain though he did not know exactly what decisions France would make on this point. With regard to
10 the troops which had retreated from Catalonia and were now interned in France he said he was making efforts to arrange for their repatriation and incorporation in the Republican army, efforts which, up to that time, had not been effective.

He continued with all the loquacity and lack of precision which
15 characterised him, to inform us about the efforts he had made for peace. He ended by telling us that he had failed in his efforts for peace and that therefore there was nothing to do but resist. . . .

After lunch the session was renewed at about four o'clock. The Prime Minister called upon General Matallana to speak. . . . He
20 spoke magnificently and gave with absolute sincerity his opinion that it would be madness to continue the struggle because it would mean much useless bloodshed. He said that since the fall of Catalonia the people and the Army had had their morale broken down by hunger and that they knew perfectly well that the war
25 should end as soon as possible. That our war industries, terribly reduced by the fall of Catalonia, were incapable of producing the indispensable minimum for continuing the struggle. Moreover we lacked raw materials . . . if we had to fight it would be with very

small reserves, with practically no artillery and what we had of
30 poor quality. The effectiveness of our airforce and tanks was
practically nil, as also that of our anti-tank and anti-aircraft
material, so scarce were they . . . Our commanders lacked the
training necessary for mobile warfare. . . .

[The Naval Commander] said . . . the Navy had decided to
35 leave Spanish waters if peace were not rapidly negotiated . . . they
did not mean to suffer the intense bombardment which Nationalist
aeroplanes made against them daily which they could not resist
because they had no anti-aircraft defence.

General Miaja, visibly excited, then said he was a believer in
40 resistance at all costs. . . . Finally the Prime Minister spoke at
length without saying anything concrete and repeated the conten-
tion that since the enemy refused to make peace the only thing to
do was to resist. . . .

The Prime Minister's attitude had made a very sad impression on
45 me and I was convinced that it was due to the work of the
Communist Party.

> Col. S. Casado, *The Last Days of Madrid* (London, Peter
> Davies, 1939), pp 118–25

(b) *The retreat of the Republican Army into France*

That afternoon the Republican troops came. They were received as
though they were tramps. . . . The Spaniards were asked what was
in the haversacks and ditty-bags they carried and they answered
50 that in surrendering their rifles they had given up all the arms they
possessed. But the French tapped disdainfully on the haversacks
and demanded that they should be opened. The Spaniards did not
understand. Until the last moment they persisted in the tragic error
of believing in international solidarity. . . . The dirty road on
55 which the disarmed men stood was not merely the frontier between
two countries, it was an abyss between two worlds.

> Regler, *The Owl of Minerva,* quoted in P. Preston, *The
> Spanish Civil War*, p 166

Questions

a In what ways does the writer of extract *a* betray his disapproval
of Negrin's strategy?

b Examine the strengths and weaknesses of the arguments
presented in extract *a* for continuing or ending the war.

c Comment on the effectiveness of the style used in extract *b*.

★ d In what circumstances did the Civil War finally come to an end
in March 1939?

7 Reasons for the Nationalist success

(a) General Rojo explains the Republican defeat

Military science and the art of war were the guiding principles of Franco's triumph. We lacked resources to continue the struggle and our technique was faulty in every echelon. Politically the Republic lacked a purpose worthy of a people striving to determine their
5 destiny. The Red government did not control the nation. Our mistakes in the diplomatic field gave the lead to our opponents even before our front began to crumble. Franco's moral stature was higher than ours at home and abroad.

Quoted in Bolin, *Spain, the Vital Years*, p 321

(b) Trotsky on the reasons for the failure of the Republic

Franco needed help from the opposite side of the battlefront. And
10 he obtained this aid. His chief assistant was and still is Stalin, the gravedigger of the Bolshevik Party and the proletarian revolution. The fall of the great proletarian capital, Barcelona, comes as direct retribution for the massacre of the uprising of the Barcelona proletariat in May 1937. . . .
15 The Popular Front resorted to demagogy and illusions in order to swing the masses behind itself. For a certain period this proved successful. The masses who had assured all the previous successes of the revolution still continued to believe that the revolution would reach its logical conclusion, that is, achieve an overturn in
20 property relations, give land to the peasants and transfer the factories into the hands of the workers. . . . But the honourable republicans did everything in their power to trample, to besmirch, or simply to drown in blood the cherished hopes of the oppressed masses.
25 As a result, we have witnessed during the last two years the growing distrust and hatred of the republican cliques on the part of the peasants and workers. Despair or dull indifference gradually replaced revolutionary enthusiasm and the spirit of self-sacrifice. The masses turned their backs on those who had deceived and
30 trampled upon them. That is the primary reason for the defeat of the republican troops.

Article written in February 1939, quoted in Cunningham (ed.), *Spanish Front, Writers on the Civil War*, pp 366–7

(c) A historian's explanation of Franco's success

The political synthesis which he achieved among his followers was the chief factor in giving him ultimate victory. . . . If this unity helped so much to the Nationalist victory, it is obvious that the

35   disunity among the Republicans was a prime factor in their defeat
      . . . no-one was able to forge a real unity out of the Republican
      warring tribes as Franco and Serrano Suner were able to do among
      the Nationalists. Dr. Negrin did his best. But such a policy
      inevitably meant making great use of the already able and powerful
40   Spanish Communist Party. The non-intervention policy of the
      Western democracies further forced Negrin to a most dangerous
      reliance on the Soviet Union and the Comintern. It would have
      been mad, indeed inconceivable, not to make full use of the
      fighting qualities of the Communists. But this itself took Negrin
45   into what was – as can be seen more plainly a generation later – an
      impossible position.
          Finally there remains the controversial question of foreign
      intervention . . . figures are not all. It was the timing rather than
      the amount of aid which made the supreme difference in the
50   Spanish War. There were five occasions when the arrival of foreign
      aid was most critical.

> H. Thomas, *The Spanish Civil War* (London, Eyre &
> Spottiswoode, 1961), pp 610–12

Questions

a   What reasons does Trotsky give to explain the defeat of the
     Republic?

b   On what points are the writers of three extracts in agreement?

★ c   Identify the occasions when foreign aid was crucial to the
        Nationalists.

★ d   Use these extracts, other documents in the volume and your
        own knowledge, to list in order of importance the reasons for
        the Nationalist success in the Civil War.

VIII   The Legacy of the War

Introduction

It can be argued that the Spanish conflict was unimportant in determining the course of the Second World War. One can even assert as Carr does, that had the Republic won, the balance of power in the Mediterranean would have become less favourable to the allies since 'Hitler would have invaded a democratic Spain during the Second World War'. Although Spain joined the Anti-Comintern Pact, Franco prudently, from a mixture of political calculation and awareness of Spain's weakened economy, avoided being persuaded into the war on the side of the Axis, even when in 1940 a German-Italian victory seemed almost certain.

Economically Spain was devastated by the war. 'The Franco regime was committed to the maintenance of the rural social structure which had been threatened by the Republic' (P. Preston). In 1951 wages were still only 60 per cent of the 1936 level and rationing continued till 1952.

Economic privation was accompanied by repression. 'The Law of political responsibilities of 1939 made all supporters of the republic liable to the penalties of death, imprisonment or loss of employment' (Browne). Executions were still going on some months after the end of the war, and an estimated 400,000 Spaniards fled into exile.

Not till the 1960s did the economy revive under the impetus of mass tourism and its associated building boom, greater economic liberalism and trade links with the rest of Europe. Meantime, the Cold War had ensured that Spain was accepted back into the international community as an ally of the United States.

Franco established 'the most enduring dictatorship of Spanish history, a personal dictatorship which lasted for forty years' (P. Fusi). But the basis for his rule was more complex and varied than is often imagined. He governed by what has been described as 'political chemistry', holding the political balance between different 'families' or groups. Initially his regime rested on the Army, the Church and the Falange but by the 1960s it had come to depend on more modern forces, the Monarchists and the technocrats or professionals. Forces of progress had been developing even before Franco's death in 1975 and came to fruition with the restoration of a constitutional monarchy. The wheel turned full circle with the introduction of democracy and recently electoral success for the Socialists.

1 The casualties of the war

(a) Estimated casualties of the war

	Republicans killed in action:	175,000
	Nationalists killed in action:	110,000
	Victims of the Nationalist terror:	40,000
	Victims of the Republican terror:	86,000
5	Civilian deaths, e.g. due to air raids, mainly on the Republican side:	25,000
	Deaths due to disease or malnutrition attributed to the war:	220,000
	Total:	656,000
10	Republican refugees:	440,000
	Imprisoned Republican supporters in July 1939:	200,000

Thomas, *The Spanish Civil War*, pp 631–3, 575, 607

(b) Ciano describes Nationalist repression in July 1939

The problems which face the new regime are many and serious; first of all there is the so-called question of the Reds. Of them, there are already 200,000 under arrest in the various Spanish prisons.
15   Trials are going on every day at a speed which I would almost describe as summary. These are carried out on the following principles: those responsible for crimes are shot; Red organisers who prepared and led the revolution without, however, staining their hands with dishonourable offences are condemned to sent-
20   ences which vary from ten to twenty years. . . . The sons of Reds executed or killed in the war are treated with great humanity; they are mixed with the sons of Nationalists in the youth organisations of the Falange.

It would be useless to deny that all this causes a gloomy air of tragedy to hang over Spain. There are still a great number of
25   shootings. In Madrid alone between 200 and 250 a day, in Barcelona 150; in Seville, a town which was never in the hands of the Reds, 80.

Ciano's Diplomatic Papers, quoted in Browne, *Spain's Civil War*, p 110

Questions

★   a   With reference to extract *a* explain what difficulties historians would have in arriving at an accurate assessment of the casualties of the Civil War.

★   b   What happened to the Republican refugees who fled from Spain at the end of the war?

c   Comment on Ciano's view that the sons of Reds were 'treated with great humanity' (line 21).

★   d   Why was Franco so ruthless in suppressing supporters of the Republic after the end of the war?

2 Spain and the Second World War

(a) Ciano's conversation with Franco, 19 July 1939

Franco considers that a period of peace of at least five years is necessary. . . . If a new and unexpected fact should hasten on the testing-time, Spain repeats her intention of maintaining very favourable neutrality towards Italy. But Franco himself realises that
5   neutrality could be maintained only for a short time, that is to say, in the event of a short-term war. But in the event of a long war it would not be possible; events would lead Spain to take up a more definite position! . . .

Franco is completely dominated by the personality of Mussolini
10   and feels that he requires him to face the peace just as he did to win the war. . . . His journey to Rome will be an event of fundamental importance in the Caudillo's political life. He expects from the Duce, and he repeatedly said so in the conversation he had with me, instructions and directives.

Muggeridge (ed.), *Ciano's Diplomatic Papers*, pp 290–5

(b) Hitler's interpreter describes Franco's interview with Hitler at Hendaye in October 1940

15   On 23 September [1940] we were back in Berlin where, the following month, the Spanish question appeared at close quarters in the shape of Serrano Suner, Franco's brother-in-law. . . . Germany naturally wished to bind Spain more closely to the Axis; I knew too that plans were in existence for taking Gibraltar which could only
20   be done if permission was granted for German troops to march through Spanish territory. . . .

I can still clearly visualise one further remarkable scene in Ribbentrop's office. Hanging by the window which overlooked the old park behind the Wilhelmstrasse was a map of the French
25   colonial empire in Africa. Suner and Ribbentrop were standing in front of it. 'Help yourself', was in effect the gist of Ribbentrop's high-sounding words. The Spaniard did help himself. He took the port of Oran; he wanted the whole of Morocco and large areas of the Sahara and needed French West Africa 'to round off' the
30   Spanish West African colony of Rio de Oro. Ribbentrop eagerly sold the goods which did not belong to him; apparently no price

was too high for Spanish collaboration. . . . In the conversation with Suner Ribbentrop, for his part, confined himself to making certain economic requests with regard to Morocco and asked for
35 U-boat bases in Rio de Oro. . . . In response to Ribbentrop's magnanimity however, the Spaniard was quite niggardly . . . this brought the first chill to the warm friendship between Franco and Hitler . . . Hitler and Mussolini referred to Suner as a 'crafty Jesuit'. . . .

40 [In October 1940] we travelled towards the Spanish frontier. . . . Franco's train which was to arrive on the wider Spanish gauge at the next platform was a full hour late, but as it was a lovely day no-one minded. Hitler and Ribbentrop stood chatting on the platform. I heard Hitler say to Ribbentrop, 'we cannot at the
45 moment give the Spaniards any written promises about transfer of territory from the French colonial possessions . . . I want to try in talking to Petain to induce the French to start active hostilities against England so I cannot now suggest to them such cession of territory. Quite apart from that if such an agreement with the
50 Spaniards became known the French colonial empire would probably go over bodily to de Gaulle.' These few sentences showed me . . . the whole nature of the problem underlying the forthcoming meeting between the dictators and they revealed the reasons why it was a fiasco. . . .

55 Short and stout, darkskinned with lively black eyes, the Spanish dictator sat in Hitler's coach. . . . It was at once clear to me that Franco, a prudent negotiator, was not going to be nailed down. Hitler began by giving a most glowing account of the German position. 'England is clearly decisively beaten', he said. . . . Then
60 came the clue word – Gibraltar. Hitler proposed the immediate conclusion of a treaty and asked Franco to come into the war in January 1941. Gibraltar would be taken on 10 January . . . Hitler there and then offered Gibraltar to Spain and somewhat more vaguely, colonial territories in Africa also.

65 At first Franco sitting huddled up in his chair said nothing at all. . . . He then undertook evasive action similar to that of his Italian colleague at the outbreak of war. Spain was in some straits for food. The country needed wheat, several thousand tons immediately. Was Germany in a position to deliver this he asked
70 with what seemed to me a slyly watchful expression. Spain needed modern armaments. Apart from this it was not consistent with Spanish national pride to accept Gibraltar, taken by foreign soldiers, as a present. The fortress could be taken only by Spaniards. . . . Hitler's high hopes of being able to conquer Britain
75 were also discouraged. Franco was of the opinion that England might possibly be conquered but that then the British Government and fleet would continue the war from Canada with American support. . . . Hitler became more and more restless. The conversa-

tion was obviously getting on his nerves. . . .

80 Ribbentrop and Suner continued the discussion in the Foreign
Office train . . . 'Spain will receive territory from French colonial
possessions to the extent that France can be indemnified from
British colonial possessions', was the formula offered by Ribbentrop at Hendaye as the utmost concession. The logical Spaniard
85 rightly objected that Spain might then get nothing. . . . Right up
to the following morning Ribbentrop continued bit by bit to
dismantle what remained of German-Spanish friendship. He
systematically plagued the increasingly recalcitrant Spanish foreign
minister, trying to high pressure the Spaniards into formulae for
90 agreements which they persistently rejected. . . .

All the way [to the aerodrome at Bordeaux], Ribbentrop cursed
the 'Jesuit' Suner, and the 'ungrateful coward' Franco, 'who owes
us everything and now won't join in with us.' The car springs
seemed to join in the abuse.

> P. Schmidt, *Hitler's Interpreter* (London, Heinemann, 1951),
> pp 190–7

(c) German-Spanish Protocol signed at Hendaye, 23 October 1940

95 Spain declares her readiness to accede to the Tripartite Pact
concluded September 27, 1940. . . .
By the present Protocol Spain declares her accession to the Treaty
of Friendship and Alliance between Italy and Germany and the
related Secret Supplementary Protocol of May 22, 1939.
100 In fulfillment of her obligations as an ally, Spain will intervene in
the present war of the Axis Powers against England after they have
provided her with the military support necessary for her prepared-
ness, at a time to be set by common agreement of the three Powers,
taking into account military preparations to be decided upon.
105 Germant will grant economic aid to Spain by supplying her with
food and raw materials so as to meet the needs of the Spanish
people and the requirements of the war.

> Quoted in Delzell, *Mediterranean Fascism*, pp 322–3

Questions

a Who were Petain (line 47) and de Gaulle (line 51)?
* b Using these extracts and your own knowledge explain the
importance of Gibraltar to the German military strategy in
1940.
c In the light of the information provided in extract *b* comment
on the reliability of Ciano's view of Franco in extract *a*.
d Why was Hitler in extract *b* anxious not to offend Petain and to
prevent the French Empire going over 'bodily to de Gaulle'
(line 51)?

* *e* Why would Germany desire U boat bases in Rio de Oro (line 35)?
* *f* Explain the reference to 'evasive action similar to that of his Italian colleague at the outbreak of war' (lines 66–7).
* *g* What was the Tripartite Pact (line 95)?
  h How far do you consider that Franco in extract *h* revealed his real reasons for delaying entry into the war?
  i What do the extracts reveal of Franco's character and political abilities?
  j To what extent does the Protocol in extract *c* support Schmidt's view that the meeting at Hendaye was a 'fiasco' (line 54)?
  k With what caution might a historian approach Schmidt's account of the Hendaye meeting? What other sources would a historian need to consult to obtain a complete picture of the meeting?

3 Spain after the war

(a) A Nationalist describes Spain after the war

The decade that followed the Civil War brought a series of calamities to the Spanish people. A plague of locusts and an epidemic of typhus swept parts of the country and were rapidly checked. Harder to deal with was the shortage of food which only
5   the Red zone had suffered in wartime . . . the shortage now spread all over Spain and was maintained by a ten year drought and by the scarcity of fertilisers and agricultural machinery. The outbreak of the Second World War hampered foreign trade and retarded the arrival of foreign aid which some opponents of the Allies were
10   fortunate enough to receive soon after they had laid down their arms.

Bolin, *Spain, the Vital Years,* p 335

(b) Gerald Brenan revisits Spain in 1949

In a Madrid hotel the valet de chambre had been caught by the Civil War in Madrid where his sympathies had lain with the Nationalists, yet the picture he painted of present conditions was sombre in the
15   extreme. The black market, he declared, was the only business in the country that was flourishing. Everyone from the highest authority down was in it. As he waited at the police post he would see lorries belonging to the Army or the Falange packed with black market goods pass without stopping.
20   'Spain', he went on, 'is finished. Everyone who can leave is doing so. If the frontiers were opened tomorrow half the

population would walk out. If you could find me a job in London I
would be deeply grateful.'

Like everyone else he complained of the cost of living. Actually
25 the prices in Madrid shops do not seem higher than those in English
ones and hotels are cheap. But wages and salaries are a fraction of
what they are with us. There has been a severe inflation and
everyone except the landowners and nouveaux riches are finding it
hard to make ends meet. . . .

30 One of the things that most astonishes me in Madrid is the
amount of building that has been done since the Civil War.
Everywhere one sees new blocks of flats, business premises,
ministries, mostly of a very large size . . . one has to search hard to
find any trace of the ruins of war. . . .

35 [Near Torremolinos] we had not been in the house five minutes
before Mr. Washbrook began to explode with indignation. The
robbery going on on all sides he declared was incredible . . . the
condition of the working class was intolerable. Their wages were
barely sufficient to keep them alive and the minute they lost their
40 work they starved. The folly of the Government at allowing such a
state of affairs was unbelievable. But then the Government and the
Municipality scarcely existed. This was not a dictatorship but a free
for all regime in which no-one thought of anything but feathering
his own nest. . . .

45 After tea we went out to look at the new villas that were
springing up. Marbella, thirty miles to the west, has been turned
into a fashionable plage and now this is happening in Torremolinos
too. The new fortunes made since the Civil War demand new
outlets. There is a municipal building scheme and land values have
50 soared. . . . 'The other day', said Mrs. Washbrook, 'a man on the
bus put the matter well. "General Franco," he said, "is a really great
man. He is teaching Spaniards a wonderful thing – how to live
without eating."'

How do the working class who cannot afford to live on the black
55 market manage to keep alive? One way is by having extra ration
books. New births are registered that have not occurred, deaths are
concealed and so forth. There is even a trade in ration books.

G. Brenan, *The Face of Spain* (Turnstile Press, London,
1950), pp 25–9, 101–11

(c) *Spanish politics under Franco*

Although the Army and the Church were the victors in the Civil
War, nothing is for ever. The major posts were initially held by
60 comrades-in-arms and the Church resumed its fundamental control
of much of Spanish life – the era of 'national catholicism' – but
increasingly Franco came to depend upon 'coalition management'
and 'political chemistry'. Franco held the political balance between

the various groupings or 'families' which administered Spain
65 during his rule. Francoism was never a steady state but in every
sense a movement with different factions in power during its forty
years of history. Initially the regime depended upon the institutionalised 'families', the army, the Church, the Falange (increasingly
deradicalised by its new name the 'Movement'). After 1943, when
70 Germany and Italy were emerging as possible losers in the war,
Falangists came to play an even smaller part in government and the
political families rather more. Of these families, the principal one
was that of Franco's comrades-in-arms; the second consisted of the
monarchists (increasingly important after 1947 when Franco
75 declared Spain a kingdom); and the third of the technocrats and the
professionals who emerged with the economic 'miracles' of the
1960s.

Browne, *Spain's Civil War*, p 77

Questions

a In what ways and how convincingly does extract *a* seek to
absolve Franco's government from responsibility for the plight
of Spain after the Civil War?

b Whar evidence is provided in extract *b* to show that Spain was
'not a dictatorship but a free for all regime' (lines 42–3)?

c What evidence does extract *b* provide to indicate that Spain in
1949 was experiencing the beginnings of an economic revival?

d With reference to extract *c* explain how and why the Falange
played a diminishing role in Franco's government by the 1960s.

★ e Describe political developments in Spain after the death of
Franco.

4 The war in retrospect

A *member of the International Brigades looks back*

There is no longer any point in trying to untangle the web of lies
and confusions which lay behind that ghastly civil war. It arose out
of total confusion and chaos. There were individuals on both sides
who committed every possible form of cruelty and beastliness.
5 And nobody, from either side, came out of it with clean hands. We,
of the International Brigades, had wilfully deluded ourselves into
the belief that we were fighting a noble Crusade because we needed
a crusade – the opportunity to fight against the manifest evils of
Fascism, in one form or another, which seemed then as if it would
10 overwhelm every value of Western civilisation. We were wrong,
we deceived ourselves and were deceived by others: but even then,
the whole thing was not in vain. Even at the moments of the

greatest gloom and depression, I have never regretted that I took part in it. The situation is not to be judged by what we now know of it, but only as it appeared in the context of the period. And in that context there was a clear choice for anyone who professed to be opposed to Fascism.

Gurney, *Crusade in Spain*, pp 188–9

Questions

★ *a* What do you think the writer of this extract means when he says that the members of the International Brigades were 'deceived' (line 11) in going to fight in Spain?

★ *b* Does the Spanish Civil War seem today to be as important an event as it appeared in the 1930s?